At the **Altar**
in your **Underwear**

40 Secrets to an Amazing Wedding

and a Better You

Niki:
You are important!
Be You!

At the Altar in Your Underwear
Copyright © 2012 Alexis Asbe, *www.allyasbe.com*

Cover photographs by Jon Gibb, *www.stixphoto.com*
Author photo by Dacor Imaging, *www.dacorimaging.com*
Flowers by Jinger Leonard, *www.theflowerhouse.com*
Hair and Make Up by Sarah Elaine, *www.stylettodesign.com*
Styling by Carol Valenzuela, *www.carolanddons.com*
Cake by Katrina Rozelle, *www.katrinarozelle.com*

Published by:
Blooming Twig Books
New York / Tulsa
www.bloomingtwig.com

Paperback ISBN 978-1-61343-025-5
eBook ISBN 978-1-61343-026-2

First Edition

For the Wubba and the Bean

At the **Altar** in your **Underwear**

40 Secrets to an Amazing Wedding
and a Better You

Alexis Asbe

Blooming Twig Books
New York / Tulsa

Contents

The Big Day

The Honeymoon

Preface

A note to you

My sincerest blessing to you, my reader, my friend.

I wrote this with you in my heart. The younger version of myself, beautiful, yet scared about the future and deeply yearning to be the best me, knows what you're feeling.

As you read, I hope you are able to remember that this is your moment to stand on the shore of a sacred beach and breathe in fresh air.

With each new chapter you take in before bedtime, you can close your eyes and invite inspiration into your dreams. You can awake refreshed and ready to love every part of this journey.

I hope you will read this book and remember you're not alone. You are *certainly* not alone in your worries, your anxieties or in your hopes.

Your wedding day and the days leading up to it are times of excitement, anxiety and growth. No matter how sure you are of your partner, there will be times when you question everything that's happening.

That's normal. And it's good.

When you start thinking about who you and your partner are, who you are as a couple, and what is important to you, your wedding will become less of a chore and more of a beautiful representation of your love.

Your dress doesn't have to be white. The tux doesn't have to make an appearance.

The only thing that needs to show up is you: 100% you.

Stop hiding your love behind a tulle veil and the expectations of everyone else.

Show up for your love and it will show up for you.

When you are able to look at your wedding (and your marriage) as a time to be "at the altar in your underwear," you will be able to enjoy the feeling of being vulnerable – because that's what love is all about.

I hope the best for you, no matter where this crazy ride takes you.

Ally

Alexis Asbe, September 2012

Introduction

"The best and most beautiful things in this world cannot be seen or even heard, but must be felt with the heart."

- Helen Keller

America – princesses, divas, mothers, decorators and wedding vendors – don't freak out! After 16 years of planning, decorating, and fulfilling lifelong dreams for over 3,000 weddings and parties, collecting millions of dollars to create the perfect room or bouquet, I am here to offer you some expert advice (or at least I would like to think so).

Believe me, I love a beyond-decadent party and I certainly know that no one is *really* going to be getting married in their underwear. I love the over-the-top details and enormous effort that transforms an empty space into a fantasy. I love the time and commitment, the lavishness of it all. I like piles of rose petals and rich food and gorgeous gowns that could walk in to a room all by themselves.

I am just as crazy as any fantasy-struck girl, dreaming about a big wedding or party. But there's more to it. I believe these celebrations; these rites of passage are vital to our existence. However, I, like others, get caught in the details, the stuff, and the glamour. I also believe society is trapped by the expectation that more "stuff" makes us better. The more things we own, the more things we buy, the better we are, right?

I know I am *not* the stuff, and I'm sure you know this too. So why do we focus on these things versus focusing on the love and commitment of a heartfelt wedding?

Frankly, what are we doing? Why is more stuff or a stressed-out overachieving bride attractive or cool? Why are we letting American TV exploit us for entertainment by showing them us at one of our most vulnerable times? Why have we gotten away from the real reason that we are getting married?

In fact, let me ask you. Why are *you* getting married?

Are you in love? Is it because you want to wear a really great dress and have all you peers adore you? What is the real reason?

So, what about your wedding then … is a wedding all about you? Or is it about your marriage, union, and lifelong commitment?

Weddings are rapidly becoming an unrealistic fairy tale, leaving us miserable and constantly trying to meet others' expectations.

There are approximately 2.4 million weddings in America each year. Forty-three percent of first marriages end in divorce, according to the National Center for Health Statistics.

Staggering, isn't it? I'm not done.

The United States spends an estimated 60 billion dollars on wedding and ceremony related expenses. This doesn't include an estimated four to eight billion dollars in honeymoon-related expenses and an additional seven billion dollars more on house wares and furniture during the engagement, and don't forget 19 billion dollars spent on gifts!

The idea of a wedding began before recorded history as a gathering of family, friends and two people vowing to share their lives together. Yet for some, a wedding has become one of the single most stressful events in their lives.

Wedding planning has become a big "business," but shouldn't it be a big "collaboration" instead, to create a special day, celebrating the fact that two people want to be together forever?

Don't mistake me for a dream-crusher. My sincere wish is that this little book will remind you of what is important. To help, I will offer practical ways to honor your union, creating a legacy upon which you can build a marriage.

Whether a large glitter-filled fiesta or a secret simple exchange of vows on the beach, this book is designed to help you have unforgettable moments to cherish for the rest of your days.

Peace, love, and enjoy your search for really cute underwear!

the ENGAGEMENT

1. If you give someone a ring

Piglet sidled up to Pooh from behind.

"Pooh," he whispered.

"Yes, Piglet?"

"Nothing," said Piglet, taking Pooh's paw, "I just wanted to be sure of you."

- WINNIE THE POOH

Children are my favorite people.
They trust us with their hearts.
Remember, your heart is very important
and your choices are yours.

Ally

Do not get distracted and move on to the next task at hand just because someone gave you a ring. Remember, just because you said "yes" does not mean you have to do *anything*.

You just have to decide what to say to this person standing in front of you. Some of us know instantly. Some have to be asked several times (like me). Some actually need a few days or longer to think and process.

You don't need to call everyone you know immediately.

You don't need run out and buy a big dress.

You don't need to go to the store and buy bridal magazines.

You don't have to have a specific kind of ceremony, whether traditional, non-traditional or stressful.

You don't even have to have a big celebration. (However, these are really fun, when done correctly.)

You can decide what is right for you. You can choose what is best for you and your love.

You can. Really.

This decision is one that will impact the rest of your life.

If you do decide to say yes, here are a few ways to remember this time of your life as more than just a great story to tell your friends.

Ten simple ideas... to be Mindful

- ◆ Write down the details of how you met.

- ◆ Create a soundtrack of music from the time of the proposal.

- ◆ Take lots of pictures and videos, and invest in waterproof mascara.

- ◆ Remember the date, time and location of the proposal.

- ◆ Do one thing at a time.

- ◆ Be patient.

- ◆ Be aware of why you choose to take on each task before you begin.

- ◆ When you do get your dress, have your maiden name initials sewn into the lining.

- ◆ Pray or meditate about planning your life and your wedding as a reflection of who you are right now.

- ◆ Surround yourself with support: friends, wedding professionals, vendors, therapists, and so on.

2. A cure for reality

"Lift him up. Be his best friend and his biggest fan."

- RUTHIE, DEVOTED WIFE, MOTHER AND FLORAL DESIGNER

People come with many talents; some make beautiful bouquets but few make beautiful lives. Ruthie makes both. She also makes really good pies and lives on a farm. Without her daily "Ruthie-isms" in conversation, I may have not made it through the planning of thousands of weddings, or, for that matter, my own marriage.

Ally

Car accidents, job offers, losing a job, a new baby, death, illnesses, weddings, and even marriage proposals. Any stressful situation or event can cause it. Beware of post-traumatic stress. It will set in when a huge life-changing event occurs.

All the adrenaline that helped you get through the situation is suddenly sucked out of your body, leaving you feeling lifeless and depleted. Often people can't even complete simple tasks or function normally until their physical body and emotions catch up.

The best way to overcome these depleted feelings is to simply surrender to them.

(You are the cure.)

After you agreed to get married, you might realize it's like you have just bought a farm. The dream of beautiful, sparkling clean, perfectly dressed children running through tall green grass, raising chickens, your love's baking and the smell of homemade apple pie made from your very own apple trees. Your small slice of the American dream is finally yours.

You bought the farm. In other words, he made an offer on the property. (He proposed.)

The offer was accepted.

(You said, "yes!")

Reality sets in. You own the farm now.

You said "yes" and feelings of relief, happiness, joy, hope and anxiety about the future are very often what you and your love may experience. Most soon-to-be-married couples deal with all of this as they are beginning to engage in the chaos of wedding planning.

Remember when I said, "You are the cure?"

When and if someone gets lost and loses sight of the dream or when things get stressful, this is what you should strive to do:

Love them.

Listen to their words and be a voice of reason.

Don't take anything personally.

Don't make up stories about what they are thinking.

Be brave enough to "keep your love on."

Act like the person *you* want to be married to.

Remind them of the dream.

Repeat!

Remember, reality can be overwhelming. It's always admirable to pursue your dreams, but sometimes people get overwhelmed and need someone to give them directions along the way.

Last, but not least, remember that this person has already shown up and committed to you. Even though you may have said yes, you actually have the entire engagement process until you actually seal the deal.

Be good to them and yourself. "Get your love on" for them, yourself and others.

Ten simple ideas ... to keep your Love on

- ♦ Spoil your partner with sweet gestures throughout this journey.

- ♦ Write them a love letter.

- ♦ Be happy and cheerful.

- ♦ Hold hands with your love whenever possible.

- ♦ Figure out how they define expressions of love.

- ♦ Don't nag.

- ♦ Flirt shamelessly.

- ♦ Encourage your love to do things they enjoy on a regular basis.

- ♦ Praise people publicly.

- ♦ Be silly! Find humor whenever possible.

3. Telling your tribe

"You know you're in love when you don't want to fall asleep because reality is finally better than your dreams."

- DR. SEUSS

Dr. Seuss really understood the energy and the awareness of children, didn't he?

Me? I love that children run around in their underwear without hesitation. I wish I could.

Ally

If the person you are marrying does not know you are getting married, you should probably tell them!

When my friend Chris asked me to do her wedding flowers, her groom had not actually proposed. However, she was bound and determined to get married. I don't think this actually worked out for Chris, as a few months after she put down the deposit she "rescheduled" the wedding.

After you both agree that you are getting married, this is the time to tell your tribe. Your tribe is the people who are closest to you. How you tell them does a lot to show how you honor your relationship with them. It is an art, and an act of love, all in itself.

Even if your list only contains a few people, make a list. List all the people you want to tell face-to-face, by phone and then via mail or the Internet. (I don't advise that your mother finds out while on Facebook!)

Place each person in the order in which you are going to contact them. Ultimately, those closest to you should be at the top of the list.

Whom you tell is very important. But how you tell them is also essential in honoring them. These are the people who have raised you, and they have contributed to who you are and with whom you share your life. Remember, these are the people who love you and will want to share in your joy and excitement. They deserve to be included in this life decision.

For some, your parents actually already know. If this is the case, you still may want to come together, letting them know your decision and sharing the news in person. This would also be a great time to tell the story leading up to and how it all happened.

Keep all the "groovy love" details to yourself since your grandma and your father definitely don't want to hear about this part. And your mother probably doesn't either.

If you are walking around in a daze, sporting a giant diamond ring that you could fry an egg on top of, you may be found out before you have time to make a list. Just ask people to please keep the good news to themselves until you have the chance to talk with everyone. And hurry up, because news travels fast!

Once you tell those closest to you and you get their blessing, you can gather your friends together and tell them all at once. During this gathering, you should be sure to tell your loved ones your intention and what you plan next for the wedding journey. Although this is about you, part of your identity is your tribe, your people, and the ones who love you and want great things for you.

After all of your "most important" people know, you can let the games begin and purchase billboard space or make a Facebook announcement or perhaps a simple save-the-date message will do.

Honor all those who care about you. They want you to be happy.

- Be unconventional in the way you share your news.

- Focus on how you feel about everything that's happening.

- Tell those who have made the biggest difference in your life first.

- Be authentic. Share your real feelings with the people you love.

- Carry tissue with you for a while. You're going to cry and those you tell will cry, too.

- Tell the story of your engagement. Again and again.

- Ask for their help. You're going to need it, and others will want to pitch in.

- Let your people know what your wedding's intention is.

- Be happy, optimistic and positive at all times.

- Be in the moment as much as possible.

4. The starting line

"Remembering that you are
going to die is the best way
I know to avoid the trap of
thinking you have something
to lose. You are already naked.
There is no reason not to
follow your heart."

- STEVE JOBS

*Being who you authentically are will be your
most impactful contribution to the planet.*

Ally

You are engaged, planning on getting engaged, or you want to have a wedding because you are obsessed with wearing a glow-in-the-dark white dress.

(And who isn't?)

You have suddenly found yourself poring over a giant pile of wedding magazines, reading wedding blogs during work hours, and planning out every last detail into the wee hours of the morning. Your every thought is a question about weddings.

People you have not heard from in years are reaching out to congratulate you as if you had just set a new world record.

You find yourself stressed about selecting a wedding date so that when the next person congratulates you, you can answer without hesitation and sound like the efficient, on-top-of-it bride you are.

This is the starting line.

My starting line is when I heard Dr. Phil talk about his son's engagement and I heard him say, "It is about the union, not the party."

Then I heard my "outside voice" say loudly, "Shut up!"

Inside, I felt a bit more aggressive and defensive:

Really? Are you kidding me? Did anyone else just hear him try to put me out of the wedding business? I think he is out to get us!

(I know, crazy. I was just crazy. I sound paranoid, don't I?)

At that time, I didn't understand it. Surely Dr. Phil was not from Texas, where bigger is better and there is a pre-party for every party? His simple sentence sent me into a mental fog.

My own private tailspin.

I knew that his words were speaking directly to me because they rang true on a level that I just couldn't understand. But slowly I found myself asking more questions:

> *Do the rose petals really mean something?*
>
> *How did I get here?*
>
> *Am I a wedding-stuff drug dealer?*
>
> *Who am I?*

It was the beginning of my big realization.

This was the moment that pro-
pelled me to want to redirect
people towards what is most true
and important.

Don't get all weird and freak out –
this is heavy stuff. It's hard to
realize you aren't focusing on
what's really important. (You may
hide under a blanket for the rest
of the week.)

Face it! Soak it in!

The fact that you have agreed to
spend the rest of your life with
someone is monumental.

Right?

Own it.

Take the day off work!

Really be with this, scream at the
top of your lungs, jump up and
down, giggle, laugh and rejoice!

This is huge!

For crying out *loud*, go and make out!

I am always amazed that people who have recently become engaged are able to keep it a secret. Frankly, I am not that contained or disciplined. I also realize it is different for everyone. How you choose to digest the importance of this time is up to you, of course, and my point is to really understand that this is the beginning of something very important.

Don't go numb and start booking ceremony and reception locations or piling up wedding magazines. *There is no hurry* and you will want to remember this time. Give yourself, your partner, your heart, and your soul time to be ready.

A new phase of your life is starting, and this is a time to prepare yourself mentally and physically to join forces with the love of your life.

Do not do anything until you are ready to take off on a great adventure and journey into uncharted territory.

Enjoy, and cheers!

Ten simple ideas...to remember to take it Slow

- Take a picture of where you got engaged.

- Document the first time you talked about possibly spending the rest of your lives together and how you felt (or feel now).

- Write down the details of the proposal: the scene, the way it happened, what the weather was like, what smells you noticed, and so forth.

- Don't try to be perfect.

- Be graceful around others.

- Don't freak out.

- Pray.

- Go slow.

- Be content within the moment, as opposed to thinking about how things have been better.

- Focus on being grateful.

5. Where the beautiful people live

"Positive thinking will let you do
everything better
than negative thinking."

- ZIG ZIGLAR

*The ability to think positively in any situation
is a trait that I admire most in people and
got me through a bunch of sticky situations.*

ally

One of the most important things I have learned in life is, your *perception* is your *reality*.

Whether you think you can, or you think you can't, both will come true. The advice you can take away from this is to be positive, because what you believe about a situation will come true.

From my experience, memorable people have learned how to be positive.

One of my favorite weddings of all time was held in the backyard in the midst of homemade dishes, linens, table and chairs with a handful of loving family members gathered around.

This bride and groom had very few resources and not many to celebrate with, so they invited everyone to contribute in some way.

In addition, both bride and groom had a number of personal limitations that would keep most from people leaving their house.

However, setting a clear intention and sticking to a commitment of being positive helped them create an event they will never forget.

As you may know or will quickly find out, planning a wedding is very stressful.

A stereotypical image of a stressed-out bride is found in everything from blogs and books to movies and TV shows. And on TV, she only gets the day of her dreams when she hires an extremely expensive professional team.

However, some of the most beautiful weddings are not created by top designers or wedding planners. People who know the secret of being positive can make these dream events a reality, all by themselves.

The secret is to shift your thinking, be grateful, and commit to being positive through it all.

You can do this!

Ten simple ideas... to be Positive

- ◆ Remember, no one is out to get you.

- ◆ Write down positive affirmations.

- ◆ Talk nicely to yourself.

- ◆ Talk nicely to others.

- ◆ Remember, "This, too, shall pass."

- ◆ Practice being happy all the time.

- ◆ See the silver lining of every cloud.

- ◆ Do not engage in cynical conversations.

- ◆ Keep your eye on the goal.

- ◆ Choose to be positive every day.

6. Normal is relative

> "My drive in life comes from a
> horrible fear of mediocrity."
>
> - MADONNA

Don't do what is expected. Don't be normal,
or settle for average. Be your own Madonna.
(I am not suggesting you run out and
buy a cone bra or anything,
but if you must, you must.)

Ally

I have had many brides come into my studio and say, "I want to do something completely different!"

For a designer, this was always *titillating*.

Then, after looking through hundreds of pictures, the bride would proceed to get all teary and worked up over a hurricane candle, even though hurricane candles are as common as processed white bread.

So much for "completely different!"

Sigh.

I struggled with this recurring situation. I contemplated simply removing all "normal" pictures from my collection.

I am special, unique, and – well – *not* normal.

However, being "normal" is relative, and I kept the hurricane candles.

Understanding why you are doing something is just as important as doing it. Being true to *yourself* is the single most unique trait one can have in pushing against average, boring, common or regular.

If you want to be different or if someone tells you *have* to do something, ask yourself and your soon-to-be spouse:

> *Why should I do this?*

> *What about that makes sense to me?*

> *Is there a something different that feels more like me?*

Think about your answers and then *act!* Question authority and others, but trust yourself, and don't worry about what others may or may not expect.

The choice is yours – either way is fine. Think outside the box or end up with a hurricane candle.

Ten simple ideas... to *NOT* be Normal

- Understand the "why" of any decision you make.

- Don't be afraid to ask questions.

- Pay attention to the way you feel.

- Wear something other than white (if you want).

- Have your partner involved when deciding on something that is about who they are.

- Don't worry about the latest fashion.

- Don't worry about current trends.

- Focus on what makes you happy, and not what others are expecting.

- Look for inspiration from unconventional places.

- Don't be afraid to try new things.

7. Liftoff

"If it stops being fun, we stop moving forward."

- SHERRI SILK, MOTHER OF THE BRIDE,
CO-PRODUCER OF *LOVING ON PURPOSE*

This was my very wise friend's intention and mission when planning her daughter's wedding. Needless to say, it was an amazing event for all involved.

Ally

Setting your intention is the first thing you need to do when lifting off.

You are going to need to channel your inner rocket ship. No, this does not mean going extremely fast, exploding, or taking off on an adventure (though these can certainly happen after an engagement).

It means you and your love are about to liftoff. Just like a rocket, you need to be extremely lightweight, know where you are going and have a plan. A rocket does not aimlessly propel into space without a clear plan of attack and, in your case, since you are entering the unknown, you are going to need to set your course.

You don't need to map out every detail, but, in this engagement phase, you need to set your intention. This will be as powerful as a rocket setting its course for the moon.

Intention is different than a detailed action plan or task list. It is the standard for how you choose to operate while executing the plan.

If you lack intention, you may get to where you want to go, however, the ride may not be as pleasant as you want it to be. Therefore, I encourage you to set your intention for this exciting and often stressful time.

The intention will bring you back to what's important for your wedding and what's important for your marriage.

Here are a few examples of how you can have intention:

1. When exploring the ideas of how you want your engagement to be, you can have the *intention* for it to be fun and exciting.

2. When talking to friends and family about your plans, you can have the *intention* for that to be a quality time of great memory-making.

3. When looking for answers to upcoming wedding questions, you can have the *intention* of being filled with both creativity and peace.

This is how you do it:

1. Be really clear about what you (both) want.

2. Share your hearts.
   Tell *others* what you want.

3. Every day, do something that reminds you of your intention.

Every couple has a unique desire for how they would like to see their engagement and wedding planning actually transpire.

There are no *right* ways.

You simply must decide what you want and how to get there.

Ten simple ideas... to stay committed to your Intention

- Be fun!
- Focus first on things that make your heart happy.
- Include the people who are important to you.
- Don't engage in negative conversation or thoughts.
- Embrace every moment like a child.
- Be playful.
- Focus on the goodness of each moment and of each experience.
- Make a sign of your intention and hang it on your (and your love's) bathroom mirror.
- Surround yourself with people who want good things for you.
- Practice random acts of kindness.

8. Gratitude is how you get your groove on

"Be thankful for what you have; you'll end up having more. If you concentrate on what you don't have, you will never, ever have enough."

- OPRAH WINFREY

I just love Oprah. I am so grateful for how she has had the courage to honor her spirit, herself and ultimately all of us. This is how you change the world. Imagine if we just applied her quote to your wedding.

ally

I don't like lima beans.

I have no idea why God put them on the planet. Lima beans taste like bad beans filled with baby powder. Really, when was the last time you had a lima bean?

This is where I shift into the mind-set I call "getting my groove on."

When confronted with fresh lima beans, I am at least *somewhat* grateful that their color is *somewhat* appealing. I simply choose to focus on anything good that is going on.

During this time of planning and preparing your wedding, it can help to look at some part of whatever is distressing you and find the one thing that you can be grateful for.

No, you will not necessarily need lima beans when planning a wedding. But you will need gratitude.

Lots of it.

(Whipped cream also helps!)

Gratitude is the single most important ingredient you will need in planning your wedding and your life.

Gratitude is the key that schools don't teach (but they should!), as a way of unlocking the equation to happiness, freeing yourself from stress, and honoring others.

When you focus on what you are grateful for, as opposed to your problems or your fears, you will literally shift your atmosphere and the atmosphere for those around you into a place of love.

(Just like I try to focus on the vibrant color of fresh lima beans.)

When you focus on stress, fear and worry, you will be stuck in a virtual dead-end or, in my case, Lima Bean Hell.

When you are feeling overwhelmed, change the feeling by focusing on how grateful you are that you have just decided to make a life with someone.

When you are feeling like you are anxious or worried about the future, focus on being grateful for the moment.

Perhaps, think about your physical health and be thankful you have a body that serves you, people who love you, a great dog, a career that you love, the fact that you are getting married, and so on.

You get the point, right?

(You can also go to the refrigerator and hopefully find some whipped cream, as I might have mentioned before!)

When you are stressed about upcoming wedding questions and all the madness that comes with it, stop and focus on what you are thankful for.

Whatever situation or problem you may experience, your gratitude will change your perception and the situation. Your beauty, your sanity, and the way people feel, all of these things depend on how you show gratitude. So get your groove on and get grateful right now.

Even if gratitude feels forced, realize that, just like a muscle, it needs time to get stronger. And each time you practice gratitude, you will become a little stronger and more grateful.

One very important tip: whatever you do, do not eat lima beans (or eat too much whipped cream). I can assure you that neither will help you get your groove on.

Especially the lima beans.

Ten simple ideas... to get your Grateful on

- ◆ Tell people how grateful you are.
- ◆ Write your future in-laws a thank-you note for raising your love.
- ◆ Start a journal of all that you are grateful for.
- ◆ Do not whine or complain.
- ◆ Be playful and look at things as if you were a small child, as if seeing them for the first time.
- ◆ Start a daily video journal and say what you are grateful for each day.
- ◆ Do things that make you feel good and lift you up.
- ◆ Laugh as much as possible.
- ◆ Follow your gut feeling.
- ◆ Look for the good in everything and in every situation.

9. Leopard print or bust

"Be yourself; everyone else is already taken."
- OSCAR WILDE

Unique people change the world.
If you don't know who you are,
this is a really good time to figure it out.

Ally

We all know women who wear leopard shoes, the matching belt, the big fat animal print purse, leopard bangles, leopard earrings and sunglass case to boot, right?

These people terrify me.

Somehow they get out of the house not realizing people will be worried that they might pounce.

These people genuinely don't care and really believe they have it going on. They are really good with who they are. This can be a very powerful lesson to the rest of us.

No, don't go out and buy animal print – that's not what I meant. Being who you are means you are able to hear your own thoughts, have your own vision, create your own memories, and be your own inspiration.

You don't have to do anything because "it is just what is expected," and you don't have to follow every wedding tradition because it is what has been done for years. You can pick and choose based on what pulls at your heart and what makes you feel the most joy.

Audrey Hepburn is memorable because she made choices that were not what people expected, but choices based on what she loved. She was being who she was. Guess what? Most of the world remembers her because of this.

Don't be tricked into doing what every other bride has done.

Honor who you are by giving yourself permission to not be too matchy-match, but instead, to make an impact by having the courage to be you.

Stay away from mainstream expectations, and remember that even leopard print is acceptable when it's truly expressing who *you* are.

(By the way, does anyone know where my vintage Parisian leopard print pants are?)

Ten simple ideas... to be YOU (fiercely)

- ◆ Be brave.

- ◆ Wear something that makes you feel good.

- ◆ Don't be stuck that white is the only color you can wear.

- ◆ Don't let people change your mind.

- ◆ Plan your wedding on a weekday or any day that is special to you.

- ◆ Let your childlike side out.

- ◆ Be quirky.

- ◆ Make up your own tradition.

- ◆ Incorporate your heritage into your wedding.

- ◆ Don't make who you are a matched set of everything.

10. Little Miss B. Little

"Be happy."

- A WOMAN NAMED GLORIA

*I will never forget reading these two words
on one of our wedding gifts. It was so simple,
yet so profound. Just be happy.*

Ally

Let's just pretend you are Miss Chicken Little. You are engaged to Mr. Big, (seems normal, right?) and you are running around professing that the sky is falling.

"The sky is falling, the sky is falling…"

Miss Chicken Little is kind of a downer, if we're being honest here.

If you want to have a memorable wedding experience, becoming aware of your negative thinking (or that you are running around like Miss Chicken Little) is the first step to overcoming it.

When you become mindful that the "little" voice in your head starts down the doomsday trail, you can turn yourself around.

When you find yourself in the Land of Little, you can make the decision to get out of there. But *only* if you know where you are in the first place.

Miss Chicken Little had a very difficult time being in the moment.

(What bride wants to hear that piece of advice: just be in the moment? You have *at least* 160 things to do to, people to round up, for an event for hundreds of people.)

However, Miss Little is here to distract you, and she *will*. When she shows up, the best way to eliminate her ranting is to shift your thinking into the moment.

Whether you are washing your hands, doing laundry or planning an epic menu, think only about what is before you.

Focus on the way something feels in your hands, the colors around you, what smells you can pick up or, in Miss Chicken Little's case, the grass between her toes. Stop and smell the proverbial roses already!

You are about to start planning a great adventure, but not for those like Miss Little. You are going to need your game face on, not your head buried in the sand.

Channel your inner warrior by staying present in the moment, swift in your step, intentional in your moves, and focused on your mission.

If you find yourself with Little on the brain, notice that she is just that: Little Miss Little in the land of little with little to say.

You have no time for little!

So let's get to work!

Ten simple ideas... to be aware of your Little thinking

- ◆ Be in the moment.

- ◆ Notice when you become negative.

- ◆ Be with people who help you look on the bright side.

- ◆ Be grateful for the little things that make you happy.

- ◆ Make a plan.

- ◆ Work your plan.

- ◆ Practice refocusing your thoughts to good.

- ◆ Never say anything negative.

- ◆ Be intentional in every task you are doing.

- ◆ Share your happiness with others.

PLANNING

11. 70 billion dollars later

"You wouldn't worry so much about what others think of you if you realized how seldom they do."

- ELEANOR ROOSEVELT

If we all learned to not worry about what others think we would all be a lot happier. When I was younger, I was tortured by it. I find the older I get, the less I care about what others think.

ally

This is going to be a really simple chapter. It is not brain surgery. These are just the facts.

You should be aware of the following things not only when planning your wedding, but also when you are making life decisions.

- People will judge you.

- People don't care.

- You don't need everyone to like you.

- You can't do anything to change it.

- If you plan your wedding worrying about what everyone thinks, it will be a big fat mess.

- The only people who matter are you and your people. (Mothers, who use this at a guilt trip, please get a shrink.)

- If you don't believe me, then it is worth addressing why you care.

If you are one of the many who do care or subscribe to doing things because "it's what people expect," I would suggest you stop reading this book now.

For those of you who are still with me, have you heard of Elvis, Lady Gaga, Frank Sinatra, or, perhaps, the Beatles?

Of course you have.

They all possess the mindset of: "I do not give a *bleep* about what you are thinking."

Do you get it?

We don't get to decide what people think. We only need to worry about what *we* think.

We do have to consider those we love and who love us, but *bottom line*, you must not plan your wedding worrying about what people think, will think, might think, expect, might expect, don't expect or may be anticipating.

This is how the wedding business became a 70-billion-dollar-a-year business. People worry more about what other people are thinking, doing, or have done that they think about what is true for them.

So, what do *you* think?

- Write a story about the ideal theme for your wedding.

- Ask your partner what they want.

- Listen to your partner when they tell you what they want.

- You can speak the truth and not be a bitch.

- If wedding traditions are not meaningful to you, don't do them.

- Walk down the aisle to something besides, "Here comes the bride."

- This is a good time to show people who you really are.

- Be your weird self.

- Be true to yourself. (Tell your Mom you love her, but ask her to have a seat, especially if she is trying to drive the bus.)

- Don't just have cake because it is what everyone is expecting. Have whatever kind of dessert that is you!

12. Village people and underwear

"Vulnerability is the birthplace of creativity, innovation and change."

- BRENE BROWN

Every time I presented a box of bouquets to a bride and her entourage, I felt as though I was standing in my underwear. This is the most vulnerable feeling, to show someone what you made just for them and hope that they love it. Remember you are not alone, when you are at the altar in your underwear.

ally

The average wedding has 160 items on the list of things to do. Notice I said, "average." Yikes is right!

It's crazy-making, especially in today's age of "download an app and get it done in five minutes."

Since each task ranges from 30 minutes to eight hours to complete, creating a wedding takes a village. This village is compiled of family, friends, hired professionals, ministers, therapists, beauty specialists, culinary experts, florists and designers (that would have been me) and more.

(Yes, I said therapists. Look back at the crazy-making comment.)

If you feel defensive, questioning, stunned, or angry at the idea that you need help, you may already be in need. Do not skip to the bottom of this page or ignore the feeling. Stop trying on dresses and thinking about ballroom dancing lessons and go directly to your favorite browser and find a counselor and wedding planner.

Do not pass Go!

Let me repeat: Go directly to your favorite resource and get some help.

Some friends in your circle who think they can do it all must be motivated to make the rest of us more normal folks look bad. Don't be worried about that, and remember they are hiding behind some bravado that makes them incapable of asking for help. Standing in the middle of the bravado will make one intensely aware that none of us are islands and we are not meant to do things alone.

What makes a great village is the resource of talent hidden within it. Honor yourself and your people by allowing them to share their talents.

This means you should recruit or hire yourself some help!

Get on with your bad self and ask for help.

And *remember*, the type of people who put their hearts and souls into once-in-a-lifetime events will be standing at the altar in their underwear with you. They will be sharing their love, their craft and baring their souls for all to see.

- Don't take people's talents or contributions for granted - ever.

- Don't be late when meeting people who are helping you.

- Show your appreciation by sharing your excitement for their work.

- Consider your sanity before deciding to do it yourself.

- Don't hire out paying attention to your partner.

- Be polite - always say thank you.

- Send honest feedback and thank-you letters to all you meet with.

- Trust your gut feeling when deciding who you feel will best honor your needs.

- Behave like a normal human and treat everyone with respect.

- Do not carry a big stick and expect people to perform.

13. Getting unstuck

"Creative thinking inspires ideas.
Ideas inspire change."

- BARBARA JANUSZKIEWICZ

My creative mind requires constant refilling or else the ideas I need aren't there when I need them. (And believe me, I need filling regularly.)

Ally

About eight years into my designing wedding days, I realized that most things that people want to create are not original ideas but a variation, or are inspired by something they had seen or experienced.

This was a huge reality check for me. All along I thought you wanted something different and unique.

I think it's funny when people say they want to be creative. Really? I know some people who have made up some of the most creative excuses to get out of work, and yet, these are the same people who think they need to call on others to help them with creative problems.

Everyone embodies his or her own creativity.

Some call it a personal style, or their look, an essence of themselves. The issue is that we sometimes get stuck.

Maybe it's not a matter of being creative, but that you're out of practice or living in a very sheltered environment or afraid to try new things.

Your wedding is the *ideal* time for you to flex your creative muscles, even if they're a little underdeveloped.

If being creative doesn't come naturally, you need to find ways to poke it a bit to see if it will come out to play.

You need to call up creativity's best friend: inspiration.

If you think you haven't met inspiration before, think again. This friend gets around.

This is the tap on your shoulder or the gasp that comes from your mouth unexpectedly when you see something beautiful.

Remember this feeling.

When planning a wedding, it can seem as though there are so many beautiful things around you, things that should all be inspiring, but you may just have moments of *meh*.

(I hate these.)

It happens to the best of us. More than I would like to admit.

To make sure you have more moments of WOW and less moments of *meh*, you need to think about what excites you.

You need to also step back from what is expected, bridal magazines, and people telling you what they think and connect back in with what is truly you.

You need to inspire yourself to inspire yourself.

(Deep, isn't it?)

Most of the time, this begins with becoming quiet again so you can *hear* inspiration in your ear and in your heart.

How can you become quieter with yourself? How can you find stillness so that you can *hear* what truly makes your heart sing?

You need to stop for a moment.

You need to be slow.

Give yourself the time you need to have that spark of inspiration, to find those things that make you feel joy and that make you feel alive with possibility.

Maybe these moments don't make sense, and that's okay. Maybe you want to have a petting zoo at your wedding for the children to enjoy because you used to enjoy that as a kid. Or perhaps you need to incorporate more nature into your planning and your big day.

Maybe.

Remember you are a creative soul with lots to express. All you need now is the push that fills your planning with gasps of joy.

- ◆ Put away the wedding 'stuff' once a week for an entire 24 hours.

- ◆ Daydream every day.

- ◆ Play music that makes you happy.

- ◆ Get out the markers and paints and make something.

- ◆ Create a collage of things that make your soul sing. It does not need to be wedding-related.

- ◆ Write down everything that makes you happy, even the small things, even the silly things.

- ◆ Talk with your partner about their ideas. They may just inspire you and remind you of what makes you smile.

- ◆ Carry a notepad with you to collect new inspirations.

- ◆ Take out an audio recorder and just talk to yourself about what you love.

- ◆ Do things that excite you or that connect to your spirit – i.e., walk in the woods, sing a song, go skydiving, dance your heart out, buy new underwear, and so on.

14. Eating an elephant

"A journey of a thousand miles begins with a single step."

- TAO TE CHING

Even the smallest steps will get you to your final destination. It just takes more steps to get there. The most important thing here is to focus on each "single step."

ally

Huge binders and countless lists of potential and actual things to do would plop on the counter as each bride sat down to plan her dream day with me.

Just the weight of these binders made me feel heavy beyond belief.

Just the idea of carrying these binders around makes me want to take a nap, certainly not effortlessly plan to walk a thousand miles.

Thankfully, your wedding isn't going to be a thousand miles – unless it's a destination wedding. (But in that case, an airplane will do the heavy lifting.)

At first, when you're thinking about a wedding and you have the list of 160 different things to do *right now*, you may begin to feel as though your head is going to explode.

Nothing seems rational or reasonable. All you can see is a never-ending list that you have to accomplish in a time that seems to be too small, too inconvenient, and too quick.

Breathe for a moment.

Lovely.

When you want to hide, when you want to run away – don't. Just be present in the moment. Let whatever feelings want to be felt, be felt.

Stay mindful and stay present. (This part can be challenging if you are having a panic attack.)

Remember, you can only do one thing at a time. And eventually, you'll get that "elephant" eaten.

You need to take small bites, and eventually, you'll eat that sustainable protein snack.

Go back to your intention and to the reasons why you're getting married. You're not getting married so you can say you checked off this list of things to do.

And you're not getting married in order to show everyone that you can get everything done on that list.

Instead, think about the ways that you can fit in smaller steps to your daily life. Check off one item a day – just one item. You can fit that in without getting overwhelmed in the rest of your life.

The best way to eat an elephant is one bite at a time.

What you'll find when you start checking things off your list is that the more you check off, the more inspired you are to check off more. And then you'll check off more.

Just a few bites into the "elephant," with a little discipline, you'll feel so good about yourself that this list is suddenly disappearing before your eyes – you will feel *good* about it.

It's crucial that you eat your wedding one bite at a time, and plan when you are going to devour each tasty little bite.

(Except at the cake-tasting. Eat all you want. This is cheaper than therapy.)

Ten simple ideas... to help you Bite off what you can chew

- Make a list of the things you need to do.
- Resist the temptation to multitask.
- When you have five minutes to spare, be in the moment.
- Focus on completing one task item a day.
- Cross the items off to show your progress.
- Break larger tasks up into smaller pieces (easier to "chew").
- Don't focus on how much there is to do.
- Ask for help if you get overwhelmed.
- Delegate tasks to professionals, or your people who are willing to help.
- Put small tasks on your calendar.

15. Your story starts here

"The best thing about the future is that it comes only one day at a time."

- ABRAHAM LINCOLN

You need to know where you've come from, in order to know how far you've come.

ally

You know those incredible moments when you find a small memento, note, or letter you saved? Think to the future for one moment.

The smells, the memory, and the feeling of these sweet or stressful times will carry you right back to that moment in time.

Gratitude and the beauty of perspective will wrap its arms around you, bringing so much understanding that you just smile with a peace that surpasses all.

This is what I am talking about!

Imagine your (future?) son or daughter knowing you in this way - if even for just a moment?

The days leading up to your wedding may not seem like something you want to document. After all, do you *really* want to remember the stress, the anxiety, and the late-night trips to the grocery store for ice cream – the only thing that can soothe your ragged planning soul?

No.

But you're also not going to get this time back. Right now, you're learning how to love this process and how to make things more graceful and peaceful – for everyone involved.

It's important now to have a way to document what you're doing, what you have done, and what you're going to do, so that you can look back and remember the feelings, joys, successes and challenges, and see how far you have traveled on your journey.

It will be staggering, baby.

Writing down or taping yourself on video talking about what you're doing, how you're feeling, and what you're thinking can be a fantastic gift to yourself and to your family in the future.

Life is worth documenting.

Let me repeat, *your* life is worth documenting.

This is only the beginning.

So start now!

Stop and think about what you want to remember about these moments as they move closer to the wedding day.

Even just five minutes a day of talking to a video camera can reveal to yourself (maybe a little way down the road) what kind of person you were at the beginning, and where you ended up in the end.

Not only are you going to have a ring on your finger, but you're also going to see how you have, in a certain sense, birthed a wedding into reality.

(Note: a *huge* accomplishment that could be wildly transforming.)

Every day is an important day.

No matter what age you are, you may not realize now that these memories are a part of who you will become.

Take time to document the journey, because the steps you take are leading you on a new path to a life that beckons to be remembered.

Ten simple ideas... to tell your Story

- Start a wedding journal.

- Document your feelings on video (much easier than writing out your feelings on paper).

- Ask yourself what is happening in your life right now.

- Talk about your successes.

- Share how others have made you feel.

- Write a letter to your fiancé to give to him on or after the wedding day, sharing all of the feelings you had before the big day.

- Write a love letter to your parents for them to open on your wedding day, praising them for all that they have done.

- Be yourself. Show the good, the bad and the ugly (which will be beautiful in the end).

- Praise yourself for how far you've come – reward yourself. (Again, cake or whipped cream works wonders here.)

- Document all of the moments, because it's not just about the wedding day – it's about the story of a lifetime.

16. Get a little drunk;
Edit sober

"As long as we dare to dream and don't get in the way of ourselves, anything is possible – there's truly no end to where our dreams can take us."

- HILARY SWANK

With the end in mind, the steps become clearer to picture and easier to take.

ally

I t's no surprise that your mind might be a little full right now, spinning with ideas, with words, with expectations (yes, those, too), and with dreams.

I recently found the story I wrote one lonely, pathetic night, huddled up on my couch (with a big glass of wine), trying to make sense of what would be a beautiful day and a reflection of us.

17 years later, it is one of my most cherished keepsakes from our wedding.

It was short, but sweet, filled with our fantasy of what our guests and we would experience from beginning to end.

It is filled with what we hoped the weather would be like, the smells of each location, the sounds and music that would create the scene, what guests would see, how they would be greeted, the mystery and beauty of it all, and let's not forget, what we would taste.

Close your eyes and think about your wedding day.

Picture what the guests will feel when they walk into your location.

What will the weather be like?

What are you wearing?

Picture the smile or your love's face.

What are your people dressed like?

See your parents' joy.

Is water moving? Are leaves blowing? Do guests smell the historical old wood in a quaint rustic chapel?

What are your best friends doing? What will they see? What will they experience? What will they be drawn to? What will they need to completely enjoy themselves?

Allow all of your senses to be a part of this daydream, finding yourself in the magic of the day and how it envelops everyone who is invited to be present to bless your marriage.

After you've done this, write down all of these details, the ones that stood out for you – especially the ones that surprised you.

When you have captured these ideas, much like catching fireflies in a jar, you have the elements that you can then add to your wedding. You have the ideas that will create the experiences that you felt in your mind and in your heart.

This isn't a time to think about what *everyone else* may think you should do. Think about what *you* want to express, and how *you* want others to feel.

This is your gift to those who are there to share in this incredible day.

Focus your thoughts on the actual wedding day, not how you will get there. Allow the dream to fill your mind.

Don't judge the ideas as they flow into your mind, just focus on watching them play out.

Perhaps you see things happening at a certain time of day or at a certain location (that you haven't booked yet), or perhaps you see the entire wedding as a certain season.

No matter what you see, capture this and picture it in your mind. Play it out in the mind when you have questions about what to do next in your wedding.

Whenever you get stuck on something to do, come back to the way you want people to feel.

When you pull at the heartstrings of others, all of your ideas will be perfect for you.

And for your day.

Ten simple ideas... to dream Big

- ◆ Close your eyes once in a while.

- ◆ Focus on how you want people to feel.

- ◆ Think about how you want to feel at your wedding.

- ◆ Let every idea be right.

- ◆ Write down the elements in your vision.

- ◆ Come back to your vision when things get hazy during planning.

- ◆ Be quiet enough, be slow enough to feel your wedding arise in you.

- ◆ Make a collage of your vision and put it somewhere you can see it.

- ◆ Go to your wedding location and visualize the day, read your story out loud to your love.

- ◆ Be inspired while in the moment and make adjustments as you become more stirred.

- ◆ Remember who you are together and individually.

17. Think tanks and throw pillows

"Everyone drops like flies
once you get engaged."

- A WISE MOM

My childhood friend's mom was brilliant.
When she said this, I thought she was crazy.
I now know how she knew this. But back
then, I thought she was crazy. (Once you
begin to realize you're not alone, you realize
that your support is not everywhere,
but in special places just for you.)

Ally

Maybe it's just me, but it seems like the second anyone gets engaged, everyone else seems to get engaged, too.

At first, that can be a little disheartening (after all, you may have wanted to be the only one), but then you begin to realize something greater, something that's more important: You're not alone.

And you begin to realize that this day is about more than just you and about having 'your' day. This is a day when you celebrate your love and when so many other people will be celebrating the coming together of their love as well.

It may be a better idea to look for a separate small group that isn't as invested in the outcome of your wedding as you are. These would be people that are not going to run when they see you as the wedding draws closer.

Businesses have the right idea with think tanks, those groups of people who come together to come up with great ideas, even if they're not going to be a part of the actual manufacturing process.

These people are objective – and you need those people in your life.

Starting a group of people who will help you get unstuck when you feel stuck, who will be objective, and who will offer support, is a great step toward not only feeling more focused, but also feeling more motivated.

You need to choose people who can be objective (i.e., folks that aren't in the wedding party) and people from whom you can feel comfortable taking advice, repeating that advice back, and then choosing the right steps for you.

(A wedding planner will not hate you in the end. They live for you vacillating and being emotional. Besides, you pay them.)

With a clear direction from this wedding focus group, you can stay motivated and you can stay on track.

You'll need the support.

(And yes, you can still update your Facebook status. But talk about your joy instead of your plans.)

Ten simple ideas... to create a Support group

- ♦ Remember that you're not the only one on your wedding day.

- ♦ Congratulate others who have recently gotten engaged.

- ♦ Find people who can support you with planning, people who are not your closest friends.

- ♦ Find an online group, wedding planner or email group to talk with about your ideas.

- ♦ Listen to the advice you receive.

- ♦ Repeat back advice to be certain you understand what is said.

- ♦ Come back to the group with what you have done.

- ♦ Be accountable to the group in your actions and decisions.

- ♦ Remember that two/three/10 minds (not bridesmaids) are sometimes better than one.

- ♦ Be sure to give back. Remember, "You get what you give."

18. Is J-Lo in the house?

> "Ally, we are going to have to teach you how to do rapport."
>
> - CAROL CARPENTER AYALA, MY MENTOR

This is what a mentor of mine said to me when I was young and brash. Basically, this is where the metal meets the road. With a good list, a few good men and women...and with a little help from above, I learned to be nice.

Ally

Remember the movie *The Wedding Planner?* I love this movie because Jennifer Lopez is an over-the-top planner who overlooks her own feelings and pours herself into everyone else's lives. This is what wedding people do; that is, the good ones. And there are bad ones. But I can assure you people who are successful at doing weddings and event planning are usually Type A, and crazy about a good list.

So, is J-Lo in the house?

If not, you're going to have to get your inner "J-Lo" on.

Or hire her.

Or rent the movie, and call it a night.

The moment you got engaged, you probably starting making lists in your head. Lists of what you needed to do, people you needed to call, things you needed to buy, people you need to hire, and so on.

A wedding can begin to seem like a "To Do" instead of a "To Enjoy." I can assure you, paying someone to make your list is also an option and a big blessing!

But lists are not the worst things in the world. Lists are good, okay? So are wedding planners, florists, bands, ministers, caterers, bakers, and counselors (well, sometimes).

90% of your success is planning your progress, but what does this mean to you as the bride? What this means is that a list isn't your enemy – it's your best friend. And even if you have a planner, you will need a list.

Maybe your list won't take you out for margaritas the night before you go dress shopping, but it will still be there for you, and so will your partner. Don't forget to kiss them good night. This is something your list or your wedding planner will not remind you to do.

While there are times when you might think that the list is longer than the calendar, there are ways to make this list work *for* you instead of against you.

Instead of looking at your list as a never-ending task master, start by looking at your timeline.

Start at the end, with your wedding date. Now, scratch off the two weeks before your actual wedding day. You're not going to do anything on your list during that time.

Yes, it is possible.

You want that time to be special time, time when you can enjoy your guests, take care of yourself, and get caught up in the joy that is a wedding celebration.

Take your big list and turn it into little lists, one for each month, each week, and so on.

Start back from the wedding date and reverse engineer your loooong list of things to do.

Look! It all fits into the timeline – like magic.

And you even have time for yourself – time to be a pleasant host that honors her guests, time to spend with your love, and time to be present in the moments.

(Plus, you'll still get it all done.)

Trust me.

Once in a while, look at your lists along the way, see what you've crossed off and congratulate yourself for the things you've accomplished.

You've come a long way, baby.

Ten simple ideas... to getting it Done

- ◆ Make a list.

- ◆ Break your list into smaller lists.

- ◆ If you delegate list items to trusted people and professionals, be sure to have a follow-up task on your list.

- ◆ Reverse engineer your To Do list from your wedding date.

- ◆ Take those last two weeks *off* before your wedding.

- ◆ Do not micro-manage; however, be sure to inspect what you expect.

- ◆ Cross off each item as you're done.

- ◆ Be sure to have small rewards for yourself in the list. (A massage, pedicure or dinner out!)

- ◆ Review your lists to see how far you've come, especially when you feel there's a long way left to go.

- ◆ Be very grateful to all those that are helping you. (Yes, more than once.) Maybe take them on little more cake tasting or invite them over to watch a good movie and laugh a lot.

19. Just do it

"So, let's do this thing!"

- LINGUINI FROM *RATATOUILLE*

You can hate what you have to do,
but you still have to get it done.

Ally

You did it. You bought the bridal magazines. You didn't really know *why* you bought the magazines, but there they are, on your coffee table – glaring at you.

You started trying on dresses, shopping online, filling your cart with the things that you think should be in your wedding…only to close out the window when you saw the price. And when you realized that you weren't as sure about the choices you were making as you thought you were.

Wake up, dreamy one.

It is time to start making decisions.

This means saying "yes" and not "maybe."

This means putting your money where your mouth is.

Get it?

It's fun to fantasize about (insert your favorite celebrity), but those dreams aren't necessarily going to help you get things done.

Instead, you need to bring things back to Earth for a minute, pull those dreams out of your mind and put them on paper, where you can start to figure out what's important.

And what needs to be done.

You could spend all of your waking hours in the dream state, but you want to have a wedding now, don't you?

The fantasy time is something to cherish, to be sure. And I don't want to deprive you of that. What I do want you to know is that there are many soon-to-be married folks who don't wake up in time for their own wedding, and those tend to be the ones that end up shouting at everyone.

These are the people that are hoping for the wedding day to get here as soon as possible so it can be over.

Don't be that bride. Don't be that groom. Don't call your mother; she already has a list.

Instead, grab your dreams and make them real.

And don't forget to kiss your love goodnight.

Ten simple ideas... to just Do it

- ♦ Start with you and your love and what you need.

- ♦ Build the dream around your values.

- ♦ Give yourselves plenty of time. There is no value in rushing.

- ♦ Make deadlines on your decisions – i.e., when to buy a dress, when to decide on favors, and so on.

- ♦ Follow your deadlines.

- ♦ Start your tasks early.

- ♦ Tell others (your vendors or those helping) your deadlines so they are accountable.

- ♦ Stop listening to everyone else (except your professionals).

- ♦ Stop dreaming and start checking things off the list.

- ♦ Get out and get moving – a little exercise will do you good.

20. Love is …
crystal clear expectation

> "Just tell me what you want."
>
> - KELLY ASBE, MY HUSBAND AND LOVE

You got to love this guy. Bless his heart.
He just wants to know what I want.
Really? Isn't that sweet? The problem
is that it changes daily.

Ally

This is the best marriage advice you will ever get. It also holds true in honoring others and wedding planning. (Are you sick of wedding planning yet?) Here it is! Are you ready – I mean really, ready?

It is pretty tough – are you with me?

Let them know what to expect.

That's it.

If there's one thing that I've learned in wedding planning, it's that people want to know what the heck is going on.

Be crystal clear. Sparkly-brilliant crystal clear.

You can't hope that people understand what you mean. You can't hope that people are going to figure things out.

Think about what you would feel like if you were invited to a wedding, but there were no directions, no maps, no parking ideas, no signs, and no dress code. You would feel lost.

Even worse, guests may *assume* what you meant to say. And only God knows what will happen when people assume!

Deep down, you just wouldn't feel like a special guest. You would feel like you were just a person who might bring a gift.

Your guests can't feel like this. You need to make sure that you're communicating everything to them – what to do, what to bring, what to wear, what to expect, and so forth.

Not only does this help them feel blessed and honored, but it also helps prevent you from being the *only* person who can answer questions when things come up.

You don't need that. You need to be focused on the *marriage* bit.

From your bridesmaids to the groomsmen, the parents to the grandparents, the friends, and so on, everyone needs to know what's going on.

Not only will people feel taken care of, but the day will also go more smoothly and be stress-free.

Your guests can plan and prepare for what you have in store. They can settle into your wedding and into your celebration, because they're there for *you*.

News flash. I am now going to say something that contradicts everything the media has been selling you.

This day isn't all about you, sugar.

It is about a bunch of other people that love you and your guests need to be in the know, too. When you have everything locked in your head, or have failed to address your guests' needs and you're the only one that has the answers, ultimately you will be one they bother on the most important day of your life. You don't need that.

The only thing your guests should have to anticipate is how you are going to spoil them rotten with love, sharing your commitment and a beautiful celebration.

Remember, this isn't just about you.

- Create an information document with logistics, schedule of events, and so on.

- Share this document with everyone involved in the wedding.

- State the locations, parking, driving times and directions clearly on (or with) your invitations.

- Warn others about traffic, if needed.

- Create clear, appropriate communication between guests, family, vendors and bridal party.

- Give out details relevant to participants' roles.

- Let people know what to wear. (For example, if the reception is on grass or sand, I would like to know so I don't wear stilettos that sink into the ground.)

- Don't be secretive or plan surprises that will make others uncomfortable unless you have a plan for that also.

- Share information concisely and clearly.

- Make sure someone else has the "master" document with the details so you don't have to answer questions on the wedding day.

the BIG DAY

21. Good princess or bad princess?

"People will forget what you say,
but they will not forget how you
made them feel."

- MAYA ANGELOU

My dear friend and mentor, Carol, was a
master at making people feel important.
No matter how busy she was she always had
time to listen and acknowledge people.
Sometimes it was with time, or just
eye contact and a warm smile
and always with gratitude.

Ally

L et's get something straight right now, sweetheart. You are *not* a cake topper, and the best stylist, dress or makeover will not make you royalty.

I know, up to this day, all of us wedding professionals, bridal magazines, and websites have sold you on thinking that you're the only one that matters on your wedding day. Forgive us, *you pay us to say this.*

The most memorable women in history have behaved in a manner that honors themselves and others. I am reminded of this when I reflect back on weddings that I feel were truly a success. The common denominator is always a gracious couple.

No matter how beautiful a bride is made up or dressed, there is nothing more off-putting than an all-about-me, "I am a princess," spirit or behavior.

Please understand that *real* princes and princesses are raised to embody elegance, grace, and manners.

The following is a list of what *real* princes and princesses do *not* do.

♦ Act selfishly.

♦ Try to get attention.

♦ Be bossy or disrespectful.

♦ Behave in a brazen or arrogant manner.

♦ Treat people with disregard.

Even the most expensive weddings (fit for royalty) that have afforded the best of every wedding detail, have failed to honor their guests due to a bride not understanding their true role.

Without your loved ones this day could just be in a judge's chamber or at your local government office.

Guests matter – and they matter more than you may have allowed them to ... so far.

I often remind soon-to-be-married lovebirds that they're not an island. They can't have a wedding on their own, just as they're not going to have a marriage on their own.

You need to think about your wedding day as a day when you're hosting a big party, probably the biggest party that you'll ever throw. And just like any other party, your guests are as important as your new fancy dress.

You will be wearing that dress (remember to stand up straight) as well as the "hostess with the mostest" hat; you are the one who has orchestrated a celebration that will make everyone feel special, honored, and excited about being there to support you on this day and in the future.

Requiring all the attention just won't do.

You and your beloved will naturally be the center of attention. How you have planned, delegated (have I mentioned how important a top level event planner is?), how you carry yourself, how you interact with your love and those you have asked to share in this epic event is what will literally be the heart and soul of your day.

It is all on you and your love to step out of the *me*-reflex and align yourselves with a *we*-attitude.

It is normal to become a bit self-absorbed as you have been focused on flexing the "what I want" muscle that comes with bringing forward your creativity and thinking outside the box.

The idea of being in the spotlight for your one day of fame and spending large sums of your or your parents' 401K can blur the *real* big picture.

You are the focal point of this story, and you are a part of a larger celebration, a larger group that is coming together for one purpose – to celebrate a once-in-a-lifetime event.

As a couple and the hosts, you need to think about what your guests need from you in advance, and what will make them feel part of the cause.

Sure, your guests are not wearing the most spectacular dress like you are, but remember, they should also be made to feel like their attendance is highly valued.

Anticipate their needs ahead of time so you get to enjoy the beauty of this day. Look each person in the eye. Give them the attention they deserve, as they have carved out time and sometimes have traveled long distances to share this memorable day with you.

Ten simple ideas... to be a Royal bride

- ◆ Think about each guest's experience.

- ◆ Delegate logistics and questions to a planner.

- ◆ Inform those close to you, like your mom and bridal party, to know answers to questions and be there to assist you as necessary.

- ◆ Ask your wedding party be accessible to your guests – i.e., those who may need help walking or who need wheelchair access.

- ◆ Never rush when speaking to anyone.

- ◆ Speak kindly and slowly when asking anyone for help – especially those whom you have hired to help you.

- ◆ Always be respectful, kind and gracious to all.

- ◆ Consider your wedding day schedule (and don't keep anyone waiting on you because you may want a million pictures of yourself – do this before or after).

- ◆ Look people in the eyes; be immensely present.

- ◆ Don't forget your love is right by your side.

22. Stop should-ing

"Why are we should-ing all over ourselves?"

- CARRIE BRADSHAW, *SEX AND THE CITY*

You are unusual, just like everyone else,
and it's the "abnormal" things that
people remember ... and cherish.

Ally

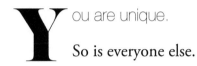**Y**ou are unique.

So is everyone else.

But you are more unique, right?

(Well, that's my story and I am sticking to it. So there!)

There's this idea among some (and I *so* want to name names) that everything needs to be just *so*.

And by that I mean there are some people who will go out of their way to make sure every *single* thing matches, from the centerpieces on the tables to the bridesmaids' underwear.

You might be thinking that if you don't have everything perfectly tailored to how your love dances (which could be necessary) that people are going to think your wedding didn't quite hit the mark.

Here's a secret: predictable is not as attractive as you might believe.

You can think that matching is stupid. You can think that white dresses are boring. You can even choose a blueberry pie instead of a wedding cake if your love wants one.

Yes, you can.

It's time to question tradition a bit and see what actually works for you and your love. Not everything will, not everything does, and I am here to tell you that "you and your love" is what makes some weddings more spectacular than others.

It's *good* to question everything. It's a great thing to stop and ask yourself if something makes sense to you and to the way you want people to feel, or if you're just doing it because Aunt Susie says you should.

As the character Carrie points out in *Sex in the City*, maybe it's time for you to stop "should-ing" all over yourself.

And all over your wedding.

I know, that just sounds yucky.

It's not about breaking rules, but about creating a day where you feel celebrated for who you are, unusual tastes and all.

Create your own traditions. This is the most important day in your life, and it should reflect what you like and what you enjoy.

True, there may be some traditions that are important to you – and that's okay too. This isn't about breaking rules to simply break them, but about choosing to be who you truly are, because you're not using the same playbook as everyone else.

The bridesmaids' shoes don't have to match their dresses. The fashion police are not going to arrest you if you don't perfectly match or if you don't have the "right" shade of lavender dyed to match the tablecloths. You can quit clutching the two-inch piece of dress fabric and holding it up to see if it is an exact match.

When it comes to "stuff," question everything that you've been brainwashed by up to this point.

The answers you get create a day that's magically delicious – and that's unusually you. It will be unique, just like you.

Ten simple ideas... NOT to be Normal

- List the things that are important for you to do in your wedding.

- List the things that are important to your love.

- Question traditions, especially the ones that you think you *should* follow. (Heck, you can question my advice too!)

- Focus on who you are, rather than how it fits together.

- Take some time to figure out what makes your relationship unique.

- Think about special symbols of your wedding — i.e., if you love pizza, maybe you want to serve pizza at your wedding or have a rehearsal gathering over pizza.

- Don't believe any of your ideas are crazy.

- Dream BIG.

- Eliminate any "should-ing" from your wedding.

- Celebrate the unusual things you and your partner like. (You'll be surprised at how many others will thank you for paving the way.)

23. Stand up straight

"Happiness depends on ourselves."

- ARISTOTLE

This day isn't just about you, but it is about how you carry yourself and make yourself known to those around you.

Ally

Everyone is looking at you. You know it. They know it. (Is it any wonder your nails are beginning to look a little chewed - okay, a *lot* chewed?)

But this isn't meant to scare you. Instead, I want you to think about how you carry yourself on this day.

There was once a bride who was also a belly dancer. She wasn't a professional dancer; she just liked to dance. When her fiancé saw her dance, he would smile and she would smile and they would share an intimate moment of love and sensuality.

On their wedding day, during the reception, a song came over the speakers and she began to dance for her new husband.

As the music and drums sounded in the hall, the guests were treated to a show of their love and their devotion to each other. To this day, this is the thing that their guests remember about their wedding.

It was simply something that made this redhead bride happy. It was a gift to her husband and it was a gift of herself. It was who she was – graceful, beautiful, and genuine.

For that moment, she wasn't a bride. She was someone who loved someone else: someone who *does* love someone else – to this day.

For that dance, she was vulnerable and beautiful and swaying to the rhythm of her love. Maybe it wasn't a perfect dance, but it created a perfect moment.

You don't have to be a dancer (though you may be).

You don't have to have a special talent to share. What you need is a way to bring happiness and joy and *you* into each and every single moment of your wedding.

Because that's what love is.

Because that's what a wedding is all about.

Ten simple ideas... to stand Tall

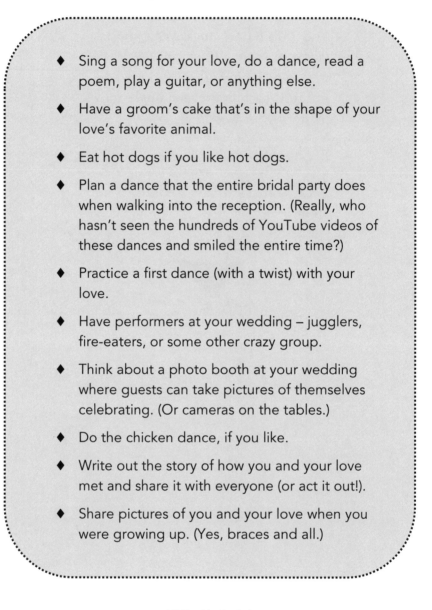

- Sing a song for your love, do a dance, read a poem, play a guitar, or anything else.

- Have a groom's cake that's in the shape of your love's favorite animal.

- Eat hot dogs if you like hot dogs.

- Plan a dance that the entire bridal party does when walking into the reception. (Really, who hasn't seen the hundreds of YouTube videos of these dances and smiled the entire time?)

- Practice a first dance (with a twist) with your love.

- Have performers at your wedding – jugglers, fire-eaters, or some other crazy group.

- Think about a photo booth at your wedding where guests can take pictures of themselves celebrating. (Or cameras on the tables.)

- Do the chicken dance, if you like.

- Write out the story of how you and your love met and share it with everyone (or act it out!).

- Share pictures of you and your love when you were growing up. (Yes, braces and all.)

24. Thunder thighs

"Family traditions counter alienation and confusion. They help us define who we are; they provide something steady, reliable and safe in a confusing world."

- SUSAN LIEBERMAN

Where you came from is just as important as where you're going after your wedding day. You can't forget the past when you're planning your future.

Ally

Though there are certain times you may want to throttle certain members of your family (wedding or not), they are still yours.

These are the people who are there for you through thick and thin.

You come from somewhere, from a culture, from a lineage, from a family name, and that needs to be a part of your wedding day as well.

For example, there's something special about a bride who wants to wear her mother's wedding dress.

(For me, even with alterations and adding massive amounts of fabric to this family heirloom, my mom's 26-inch waist prevented me from wearing my mother's wedding dress at the time.)

Remembering where you came from is an integral part of knowing who you are. It's not just about the past, but it's also about the lineage that you're creating. You're branching off the family tree, but the roots are just as important to invite into your plans.

Cliché or not, the idea of 'something old' is something special to incorporate into this day.

When you bring your history and your roots into your wedding, you thank the people who came before you and you celebrate all that they have done for you.

Also, when you bring your love's history into the room, you celebrate their family tree that brought them to you.

This day is about more than just the ring on your finger and (possibly) a new last name.

Your wedding can include everything from family recipes to family photos to ethnic music and outfits. Reach back into your history to learn more about where you came from.

Invite the past to dance with you on your wedding day. It's not going to step on your toes. It will also honor those who have come before you and possibly remind your guests of their roots as well.

If anything, a little culture will show you a few new moves that you hadn't known before.

Honor the past as you move into your future.

Ten simple ideas... to honor your History

♦ Use antiques or items from other family weddings in your décor.

♦ Utilize a unity candle that others in your family have used.

♦ Serve food that is of your love's ethnic origin.

♦ Look at how your wedding dress can incorporate your family history – tie your bouquet with lace from one of your family's wedding outfits.

♦ Ask your relatives to share stories of their weddings.

♦ Frame wedding or family photos of your relatives at an entry, gift or cake table.

♦ Celebrate your ethnicity – maybe in your dress or your jewelry.

♦ Have your wedding cake or dessert made with your family's secret ingredient (maybe you share what it is, maybe you don't).

♦ Follow a family tradition that rings true for you.

♦ Let your guests know that how the details of your wedding are related to you. Celebrate their marriages.

25. Leave room
for the in-between

"Son, on this day, remember to slow down because if you don't slow down, you're going to miss the really good stuff that happens."

- A WISE FATHER

A wedding day is just one day to capture happiness in a bottle and save it for later. Scheduling too much or anticipating what's next is going to prevent you from experiencing the really good stuff in between.

Ally

A blonde bride looked in the mirror and obsessed about her hair – it wasn't curling in the August humidity, and it *needed* to be curly.

A vision in white, her thoughts raced:

I'm not going to look good enough.

It's too damn hot.

I need a drink.

Why did we plan this in August?

What if all the guests get up and leave?

What if Aunt Madge has a heart attack?

Suddenly, she felt a hand on her shoulder.

A friend (not a very close friend, but a special friend) whispered in her ear that she needed to breathe.

The bride needed to remember that everything would go by quickly if she didn't slow it down.

She breathed in and repeated, "Slow."

The day became the day that she wanted it to be. (And her hair even started to curl.)

Trying to have everything fit in and trying to have everything be scheduled down to the second is a recipe for exhaustion and stress.

Yes, it's a good thing to have a schedule, but if you're just worrying about what happens next, you're not thinking about what happens now.

Let's break down the numbers for a minute (stay with me here).

If your wedding is at 5:00pm, your reception is at 7:00pm, and the hall kicks you out at midnight, that's seven hours for your big day.

Seven hours.

That is less than one workday.

You need to slow down, and let the experience of the day happen as it's going to happen.

Every time you begin to rush in your mind, go back to being slow.

Breathe. This day will move in the way that it needs to move.

In the network television program *The Office*, when characters Pam and Jim get married, they take fake photos using their fingers of each moment during the day, trying to capture the day before it slips away.

You can do that, too.

Slowly.

Ten simple ideas... to leave Room for yourself

- ♦ Stop and breathe.

- ♦ Leave wiggle room in the day's schedule.

- ♦ See if you can remove anything from the schedule that isn't essential to your wedding day.

- ♦ Move slowly during the day.

- ♦ Assign one person the task of reminding you to move slowly.

- ♦ Forget about perfection.

- ♦ Don't worry about what happens next.

- ♦ Avoid wearing a watch or looking at the clock. Have someone else do that.

- ♦ Schedule ten minutes for just the two of you to catch a moment alone.

- ♦ Take moments with your husband to hold hands and look around at the people around you.

26. What do you believe?

"We question all our beliefs, except for the ones we *really* believe, and those we never think to question."

- ORSON SCOTT CARD

You can show off your morals and your beliefs, and get guests involved in what's important to you. Before, during, and after your wedding.

Ally

You already believe in love – so much so that you're signing up for a lifetime of commitment to someone else.

You may not have committed to a hair color or a purse, but you have committed to something bigger than you.

But what if you have other causes to celebrate?

Even if you're not a hippie (or if you are), you can bring what's important to you into a wedding day.

From bringing in an eco-friendly theme to serving all vegan dishes, it's *your* day, so let's think about what matters most to you.

What's funny about most wedding days that you see on television is that this is a day that's not really about the couple or who they are. Sure, the wedding might be filled with things they like or that they think are pretty, but what about who the couple is when they're not in a white dress or tux?

You can let your guests know who you really are and what's important to you by embracing your case during your wedding.

No, don't whip out your picket signs, and please leave your soapbox at home (unless that's *really* important to you).

Think about what you want your guests to know about what's important to you as a couple. Maybe you just mention your cause on your program or in your invite, or perhaps it's even bigger than that.

Maybe your cause embraces your entire wedding. Have a mission and a mission statement for your wedding – one that even goes beyond love.

This wedding is, after all, about more than just you and the gifts you get from your registry.

If you spend your time thinking about bigger things and about saving the world, why not let everyone at your wedding know?

Why not make a special day even more special by helping others or by helping the planet?

That's going to create a memory that might even outlast your fantastic photos.

Ten simple ideas... to support your Cause

- ◆ Think about the causes you support.

- ◆ Consider charitable donations as favors for guests.

- ◆ Request donations for your cause in lieu of presents.

- ◆ Plan a zero waste wedding. Hire an eco-friendly planner who can choose décor and foods that will have minimal impact on the environment.

- ◆ Use cause-related colors in your décor.

- ◆ Send leftover wedding supplies to charities.

- ◆ Donate your wedding dress to someone who needs it.

- ◆ Write a small essay about why you're supporting your cause, and share it with your guests.

- ◆ In your thank-you notes, make sure to let guests know how you supported a cause.

- ◆ Have a homemade wedding that supports simplicity.

27. Give that lovin' feeling

> "We think too much and feel too little."
> - CHARLIE CHAPLIN

The precious moments in life are measured in emotions, rather than details. And the beauty of our memories is that while they will eventually fade, there is always a piece that stays in your heart.

ally

Look – we're all going to get old, whether we want to admit it or not.

We will get old, and our brains will begin to get, well, lazy. They're not going to recall the exact pattern of your wedding plates or the number of flowers you had in your bouquet. (That's what photographers are for.)

Even more importantly, your guests are older than you and they're going to remember less about the wedding details and more about the "feeling" of the wedding.

In one wedding that cost only 3,000 dollars and hosted about 100 guests about ten years ago, the one thing that will always be memorable is how the guests felt at the end of the wedding.

See, at the end, the entire wedding guest list was treated to a surprise fireworks display. For 15 minutes, everyone came out from under the tent and watched the sky light up with sound and sparkling colors.

Everyone was quiet, silently looking up at what celebration looks like.

To the day, not everyone remembers what happened at that wedding, but they remember leaving with a childlike wonder in their hearts. They felt joy and excitement and *that's* what's stuck with them all of these years later.

The bride and the groom didn't announce it. They didn't explain it. They didn't even know it was going to happen until it did.

You don't need fireworks to make your guests look up in awe at your wedding, but you do need to think less about the details and more about the feelings you can stir up.

No matter what we wedding professionals have told you, your guests are the most important people on a wedding day. Without them, the wedding would just be a long glance between you and your partner, a few words, and a kiss.

You need to behave gracefully during this day, showing that you are having a good day that is filled with happiness for your love, and for those who have made their way to your special day.

Say less, feel more.

Ten simple ideas... to give that Lovin' feeling

♦ Keep your smile on all day.

♦ Say less.

♦ Focus on your guests' experience.

♦ Surprise your guests during the event.

♦ Practice good manners. Remember, manners are designed to make people feel comfortable.

♦ Create feelings through special touches, special moments, and special wordless expressions of your love.

♦ Show your love grace, kindness and passion on your big day. Give this with reckless abandon.

♦ Express your love to your parents and in-laws on your wedding day. Give hugs, dance with them, and spend time with them.

♦ Smile!

♦ Think of how people you love make you feel.

28. In your underwear

"As we express our gratitude, we must never forget that the highest appreciation is not to utter words, but to live by them."

- JOHN F. KENNEDY

Being thankful is the primary way you celebrate. So party on!

Ally

Your life is blessed. On your wedding day, there will come a moment when you look around the room and really see this in action.

From the way that your friends are smiling to the tears in your parents' eyes, the beauty of your life and of this day will probably overwhelm you.

Let your tears fall. Mascara be damned.

This is a day when you have a perfect setting to show just how grateful you are. Thank everyone for being there. Thank everyone for being special to you.

Thank everyone more than you think they need to be thanked.

One of the most beautiful parts of weddings is the moment when the bride and the groom get up in front of everyone to thank them for being there.

This doesn't have to be a rehearsed speech, as it's going to come from your heart. Remember the title of this book? This idea of being "at the altar in your underwear" is more than just a vision you may have shuddered at when you first read it.

It's about being vulnerable. It's about being completely naked of pretense and selfishness.

Being naked is about being clear about the feelings you have and expressing them with abandon. Say what you mean, don't hold back and don't think that everyone already knows what you feel.

It's not enough to invite people you love to your big day. You need to tell them, each and every one of them, that you are grateful that they are a part of your life.

Tell them all - from the cousin who helped you fix your hair to the uncle who couldn't finish his sentence when congratulating you – of course, he wasn't crying, he said. Allergies, (yeah, *right*).

Thank them all.

Express the fullness of your gratitude and make sure that every single person in that room knows that you are deeply touched by their roles in your life – even the smaller roles that people take on.

Be grateful, darn it!

Ten simple ideas... to show how Grateful you are

- ◆ Take out the list of your guests and write down one thing that you appreciate about them.

- ◆ Write out personalized thank-you notes, even to the people who didn't give you a gift.

- ◆ Make a speech that thanks everyone for coming.

- ◆ Show how you really feel in every moment of the wedding day.

- ◆ Thank others publicly, whether in a speech, the program, or on your wedding website.

- ◆ Continue to thank people in your life, even after the wedding.

- ◆ Write down all of the things that you were grateful for on your wedding day.

- ◆ Thank your groom for his love.

- ◆ Thank yourself for the hard work you have done.

- ◆ Don't hold back anything on your wedding day. Feel free to let it all out.

29. R–E–S–P–E–C–T

"R-E-S-P-E-C-T, find out what it means to me."

- OTIS REDDING,
(AS SUNG BY ARETHA FRANKLIN)

You know how you like to be treated, and others want to be treated in the same way. With respect.

ally

For some reason that bog- -gles my mind, the idea of a *bridezilla* has become a bit of a joke.

Like it's okay for brides to yell at everyone because they're stressed out about their big days.

Give me a break!

Just because you're getting married doesn't mean you can treat others like they are your servants. Just because you're getting married doesn't mean you can yell and scream at people and demand what you want.

Puh-*lease*. I am so tired of this sort of attitude and what it's starting to breed in the wedding world. Brides who are, well, bitchy may get their way, but they're also losing the respect of those around them.

And it's sad.

Kindness can be the motto of every bride, and if you allow me to "should" on you for a second, kindness should be your attitude.

From the guests you invite to the wedding planner to the vendors, you should treat everyone with respect. This means:

1. No yelling.

2. No cursing anyone out.

3. No demands.

4. No temper tantrums.

Think about how you would respond if someone yelled at you. Even if you knew they were stressed out, it still would leave a sour taste in your mouth.

Even if you love them.

One way to approach it is to talk to everyone involved with your wedding as though the person was your grandmother. Treat them with the utmost respect and reverence.

No sassing.

Even when you have feedback to give to someone about something that's happening, ask them if they want the feedback first, then give it in a constructive way, and work together to find a solution.

The old idea that you catch more flies with honey is what I'm talking about. But it's not about manipulating with kindness.

Treating others the way you want to be treated is the lesson here. Being a graceful bride (and person) is the lesson, too.

And your mom is probably watching you on your wedding day. You don't need a lecture as an additional wedding gift.

Ten simple ideas ... to show Respect

- Use your manners.

- Say "please" and "thank you."

- Treat everyone like a relative (a relative that you like).

- Always, always, always treat vendors with respect.

- Never take people for granted.

- Show your guests respect (for example, don't keep them waiting).

- Be respectful of your groom.

- When you are overwhelmed and feel like yelling, breathe ten times, in and out, until the feeling passes.

- Be clear when you are upset, but stay calm and don't take it out on someone else.

- If you do get upset, apologize immediately and smooth things over.

30. Just one cha-cha

> "It's not what you spend but
> how you wear it that counts."
>
> - CHLOE SEVIGNY

*Standing out at your wedding seems
easy peasy, but being memorable
will take a bit more planning.*

ally

I have a friend who likes to wear what I call *cha-cha*. You know the type – the one who always wears a lot of bling.

And that works for her. She looks great.

But, that's not my style. Instead, I try to wear a *single* piece of cha-cha when I get dressed, creating a focal point: something interesting about the way I look on that particular day.

Your wedding either needs a little or a lot of cha-cha.

This cha-cha becomes a focal point for your wedding – the part people will be drawn to when they think back on that day. Whether it's a fireworks show or a special toast, you need to spice things up a bit.

One couple created a special moment during their wedding, which was taking place by a pond in a friend's backyard.

Beside the pond was a basket of floating candles, and at a certain point of the reception, the guests were invited to light a candle and send out a wish for the couple as they placed their candle into the water.

It was after dark when the candles were lit, and soon the pond was filled with bright wishes for the couple that dimmed as the sun came up the next day.

(Side note: my friends' pond, to this day, still has remnants of these candles.)

At some point during the wedding or the reception, create a magical moment – something that brings the guests together in celebration and that allows them to create something special as well.

It doesn't have to be expensive. It doesn't have to be complicated.

But it does have to be memorable.

And it will be.

Ten simple ideas... to add some Cha-cha

- ◆ Give a special toast before everyone eats.

- ◆ Perform a fun dance with your groom during your first dance. Practice ahead of time to really wow people.

- ◆ Have a way to send good wishes to the bride and groom (i.e., the floating candles idea, a wish tree, and so on).

- ◆ Schedule a special performance during the wedding.

- ◆ Ask friends to play songs during the reception.

- ◆ Offer a sundae bar with the favorite toppings of the bride and groom. (Really, how fun is that?)

- ◆ Get everyone on the dance floor (that can dance) to do the Electric Slide.

- ◆ Line dance, if you're a country gal.

- ◆ Play a video for guests to enjoy during dinner.

- ◆ Perhaps the groom might set up a surprise for his new wife (hint, hint).

- ◆

the HONEYMOON

31. Time to Rest or Collapse

"For fast-acting relief, try slowing down."

- LILY TOMLIN

If there was ever a time you deserved
a little "me" time, it would be now. Even
if you've paced yourself, the hangover
of a wedding can be overwhelming.

Ally

The day after your wedding (alcohol or not) is a doozy. You wake up with your list of To Dos done, covered in bliss and possibly a few dabs of icing on your chin.

You wake up and realize – *we're done*. Jump up, enjoy the moment, and hug your love. Celebrate. Have another piece of cake.

But since you've been running back and forth up until this point, you may not want to slow down. You might be thinking thankyounotes photospreadsthankyoupartiescallthe parentspackforthehoneymoon …

STOP.

Seriously, just stop it for a moment. You've earned a bit of a rest. Heck, you've earned a lot of a rest. You and your sweetie should take a day to just breathe.

(You did put that into your schedule, didn't you?)

Take a day to decompress, to chillax, to rest, to sleep until noon, or whatever it takes to make you feel as though you're getting a break.

And no, doing more wedding things is not an option.

You've worked hard up to this point, and while this is something to celebrate, your body and your mind and your soul need a break. You need to take a deep breath and look around at everything you've done.

Then you need to stop.

Take a rest. Make your partner take you to a hot spring or to a spa. Or rent a room in a local plush hotel and just sleep. Or read a non-wedding book.

You deserve a respite from the madcrazywonderfullyworthit rush.

I like to tell couples to schedule a free day (or two) before their honeymoon so they can rest for a bit and have the energy they want for their honeymoon fun.

And schedule a day (or two) after your honeymoon, too.

Ease back into 'normal' life. Enjoy being a couple without being back at work or trying to achieve anything.

Ten simple ideas... to help you Rest

- ◆ Unplug your phone for 24 hours.
  At least.

- ◆ Rent a room at a hotel to get away.
  Tell no one.

- ◆ Schedule couples time at a spa.

- ◆ Schedule your own time at a spa.
  You deserve alone time, too.

- ◆ Sleep in.

- ◆ Take a nap. Or ten.

- ◆ Don't go back to work for a bit,
  if you can.

- ◆ Ignore your To Do list.

- ◆ Lie in your partner's arms.

- ◆ Be completely lazy for 24 hours.
  Make it a contest with your partner to see
  who can be lazier. (Trust me, it's more fun
  than you might think.)

32. Be annoyingly appreciative

"If the sun refused to shine, I would still
be loving you. When mountains crumble
to the sea, there will still be you and me."

- ROBERT PLANT

*Gratitude should be an attitude, not just
something that you offer when you think
you should say it. It comes from the heart
and it comes from appreciating what you
have in your life because there's always
something to be grateful for.*

ally

I am a *huge* gratitude advocate. If I could, I would tattoo *thank you* across my forehead. Well, not really, but I do think we need to be more grateful.

So often, it seems we save up our gratefulness for "appropriate" times – after someone does us a favor, or after someone gives us a gift.

But really, there's more to the gratefulness story, isn't there?

If you really stopped to think about it, you could be thankful for little things too, not just the big, obvious things. Just today, I'm feeling grateful for the hot water in my tea mug.

Yes, it can be that simple.

Say "thank you" until you mean it and when I say that, I mean that if your appreciation muscles are rusty, start by saying "thank you" for everything.

Everything.

When someone opens a door for you, thank them.

When someone touches your shoulder to reassure you, thank them.

Keep saying "thank you" over and over until you not only mean it, but you also feel it.

(Hint: it feels good.)

Right now, I'm sure you can re-member a time when someone showed how appreciative they were.

Even today, you can think about that gratitude and smile.

Gratitude is a gift that you can give to anyone, anytime, for any reason. You don't need to gift wrap it, but you do need to give it away as much as possible.

Being grateful does so much more for your loved ones than fancy fa-vors ever could.

You are honoring who they are and what they mean to you. While "thank you" may never seem like enough, it's a great way to begin.

And, if you're wondering, everyone loves to hear that they're someone who is noticed and appreciated.

Ten simple ideas... to show your Appreciation

- ◆ Send handwritten thank-you notes.

- ◆ Write thank-you notes for each of your wedding party folks to read before the wedding begins.

- ◆ Give small wedding party gifts as a token of gratitude.

- ◆ Thank your vendors with notes.

- ◆ Look people in the eyes and thank them.

- ◆ If someone asks why you're thanking them, just tell them, "because of all you do for me/us."

- ◆ Write down notes of things to be thankful for each day.

- ◆ Give thank-you notes in a timely manner.

- ◆ Thank your guests again on your first anniversary.

- ◆ Be grateful and let others know that you are grateful by mentioning them in the toast, the program, the invites, and so on.

33. Destination inspiration

"Creative thinking inspires ideas.
Ideas inspire change."

- BARBARA JANUSZKIEWICZ

*You're not just a bride on your wedding day;
you're an example to others of
what needs to happen.*

Ally

Confession time. Yes, I've seen a *bridezilla* reality show or two. (I am NOT addicted. Promise.)

I've noticed something during these shows. When a bride begins to freak out and start yelling at everyone, everyone else in the family does, too.

And that's when things get crazy.

And ugly.

And sad.

I wonder what might have happened if the bride had just kept her cool. Yes, it might have been boring TV, but if the bride had set the example of grace and civility, chances are good that everyone else would have done the same.

You are the example on your wedding day, and it's a responsibility to take seriously.

That little flower girl is looking at you as though you were a princess, but if princess has a potty mouth and is screaming and crying about everything, you're not setting a good example. At all.

Even when things are getting out of control, you can stop yourself from lashing out and being a brat.

Stop and really think about how other people feel and what it would feel like to walk a mile in their shoes.

They want to be treated the way you want to be treated.

All the Golden Rule clichés that you've heard a million times, there's a lot of truth to them, even if you've learned them from greeting cards.

Now, before you start shouting at everyone, think instead about how you can set the tone. Show others how they should behave and they will follow your example.

Trust me. No one wants to upset a bride, and when others see the bride is the picture of grace, they'll want to follow your lead.

You don't have to be Martha Stewart to inspire, but you do want to find that composure that she has when she's creating something beautiful.

(But avoid the jail time, okay?)

Ten simple ideas... to Inspire others

- ◆ Move slowly all day. Take your time.

- ◆ Take deep breaths, often.

- ◆ Think about how you would want to be treated.

- ◆ Close your eyes and picture how you want to act.

- ◆ Practice being graceful and composed.

- ◆ When you become upset, think about what you can do to fix the problem.

- ◆ Remember that it's okay to be emotional, but it's not okay to be mean.

- ◆ Remember that you are being watched.

- ◆ Laugh.

- ◆ Step outside when you need to compose yourself.

34. Back to the starting line

"The achievement of one goal should
be the starting point of another."

- ALEXANDER GRAHAM BELL

*Even if you've been married before,
this marriage is different and you deserve
some time to figure out how it feels
and what it means to you both.*

Ally

The whirlwind tour of getting married has finally come to an end. The thank-you notes have been sent, the crappy gifts have been exchanged (yay for gift receipts!), and the dress is in storage.

You can go back to the way things were, right?

Sort of.

You're in a marriage now and that means things are different, even if you've been living together for years. You can feel it from the time the minister, priest, rabbi, or officiant tells you that you're legally bound to each other.

Something is different!

I don't want to sound like your mother here, but when you get married, it's a lot like having a kid.

(No rush on that, okay? You're going to learn why in a moment.)

Everyone around you is going to start telling you that there is a certain way to be in your marriage. Just as these same folks are going to tell you how to be pregnant or how to raise kids.

You're a part of a special club right now, and this is not a bad thing. But it can become a confusing thing. You've spent all of this time trying to showcase the uniqueness of you and your partner.

And now you're hearing there are certain ways to be in a marriage. Sigh.

Nope. No one's marriage is perfect or right. It might be perfect for them, but it doesn't mean it's perfect for you.

Yes, yes, I've given advice, but you should do what works for you. And not everything will.

I recommend that you spend some time just with your partner, figuring out what it means to the two of you to be married. Hide from the advice-givers and see what works for you.

You don't *have* to do anything that someone else recommends to you. You don't have to read marriage books and you don't have to listen to Dr. Phil.

You need to listen to each other now. When you do this, you start a new chapter of your life, a new story, and a new romance. You are unfolding the new path that marriage opens up to you.

♦ Have regular date nights. With just the two of you.

♦ Spend a month (or so) enjoying your time together as a couple.

♦ Give each other some space. You're both figuring things out, after all.

♦ Don't ask for marriage advice. Don't seek it out.

♦ Talk, talk, talk.

♦ Create traditions that you share as a couple.

♦ Solve problems together. You can do it!

♦ List what you love about your relationship. Share lists with each other.

♦ Spend some holidays together, on your own or by inviting others to come to your home.

♦ Enjoy each other. Just as you both are. Just as your marriage is.

35. Understanding your love's language

"If we can agree that the word love permeates human society…we must also agree that it is a most confusing word."

- DR. GARY CHAPMAN

The language between a couple is one that speaks volumes about who they are and about who they become when they are together.

ally

As you enter into the loving embrace of marriage, you need to make sure you understand what your partner needs from you. They can tell you what makes them feel loved and you can tell them what makes you feel loved.

And then you'll both know.

Trust me, when you know what the other person wants and you ask why the other person is doing what they are doing in response to a situation, you're going to have a much easier time in marriage.

Start off strong and you'll build a solid foundation of love. One that lasts longer than your honeymoon.

When people meet my husband and me, they can see that we are different. (Yeah!) It's not because of how amazingly good we look together, but that we speak to each other in a unique way.

The sitcoms would have you think that there is *one* way to speak to your partner. The woman gets what she wants or the man gets to sleep on the couch or be made fun of by everyone else.

Puh-*lease*.

The reality is that each person in each couple has different things they need from the other person. But we get stuck sometimes in thinking that what *we* want is what the other person wants.

(You can see how this can go wrong quickly.)

In our relationships, we're not just married and everything is hunky-dory. Even if you've known your partner for a while, you still need to figure out how to be the best partner possible for them. You may not know how to do this yet, even with a ring on your finger.

For example, when a person is having a bad day, one person might want to head out for a night on the town to disperse their bad juju. But the other partner might want to vent to the other person.

Both of these are good things and both of these options work, but they can lead to a communication breakdown.

Think about what might happen if one person doesn't understand why the other person doesn't want to talk about their feelings. They might see the other person as avoiding their feelings, which can cause confusion.

Ah, the languages of love.

Another way to look at translating the languages of love is to consider what your partner needs to feel loved. Some might want gifts, others might want recognition, and others may want physical touch.

Or something else.

If you don't know what your partner wants, then you're going to be sending mixed signals and your partner may not feel appreciated or cared for.

Ten simple ideas... to Speak the same language

- ◆ Ask for what you need. (It's hard at first, but gets easier.)
- ◆ Ask your partner what he needs.
- ◆ Write down your favorite ways to be cared for.
- ◆ Share what you need when you're sad/angry.
- ◆ Talk to your partner about what you could do better.
- ◆ Don't take anything personally from your partner, especially at first. They don't know your language yet.
- ◆ Practice giving what your partner wants.
- ◆ Schedule regular times to talk.
- ◆ Speak without speaking. (Hint, this involves a bed...)
- ◆ Look your partner in the eye and tell them that you love them. Often.

36. You *are* enough, darn it

"To love oneself is the beginning
of a lifelong romance."

- OSCAR WILDE

*Your marriage is a part of your life, but it is
not the entire sum of who you are and what
you have to offer in the world. You must
know that you are enough.*

Ally

You are enough. You are amazing.

This doesn't change once you're married.

First of all, I'm not telling you that your partner isn't important. Not at all.

(So, tell them to stop reading over your shoulder.)

What I am saying is that your marriage can become an excuse to be a *we* as opposed to a *me* and *you*.

Once upon a time, marriage meant women had to be the little wife who stayed in the kitchen and did everything that the husband wanted them to do.

Now, I'm not going to go all feminist on you, but what I do want you to know is that women don't need to be continuously looking to their husband now that they're officially married.

Yes, you have big decisions to make together (house, kids, cars, what to watch on Netflix), but you also have your own interests and your own life.

And you *should* have your own life. (And your own bank account!)

When you have your own interests and your own things to do, you will remain confident in the way you are in the world.

It's just too easy to say that you can't do something because your partner doesn't want to do it. Or you might drop away from certain friends or interests when you get married.

Stop it. Please.

You are enough without your partner. You can be just as amazing as you were before you married.

Smile. Be confident. Be positive about who you are and what you have to offer in the world.

Think about it this way – someone has just committed to spending the rest of their life with you. If that isn't enough proof that you're enough, and that you should be radiating confidence 24/7, then you may want to talk to a friend and have them remind you.

Yes, nothing is going to be as amazing as your wedding day (for many) and you may never feel as beautiful as you did that day, but that doesn't mean you shouldn't try to replicate this feeling.

Every single freaking day.

Ten simple ideas...

- ◆ Spend time on your own.
- ◆ Share some interests with your partner. Not all of them.
- ◆ Continue to meet with friends.
- ◆ Try new things, new hobbies, and so on.
- ◆ List the things that are amazing about you.
- ◆ Continue to try to impress your partner. A little makeup or a clean shirt goes a long way to make *you* feel good.
- ◆ Look at yourself in the mirror and tell yourself that you are enough.
- ◆ Compare yourself to no one.
- ◆ Compare your marriage to no one else's.
- ◆ Smile.

37. Reinvent yourself again

"And as I reinvent myself and I'm constantly curious about everything, I can't wait to see what's around the corner."

- PAM GRIER

Marriage should not be an excuse to stay exactly who you are. It can be a stepping-stone to becoming an even more amazing version of yourself.

Ally

Some couples irritate me, even from the time I meet them in a wedding planning appointment. Why? Because I can see one of them already starting to freeze in time.

It's almost like they realize that they are being married as the person they are and they don't want to change.

It's fear that's driving their marriage. Bad. Bad. *Bad*.

I want you to know that marriage isn't an excuse to never grow or change again. Can you imagine being with your partner forever and them never changing?

No. So why are you planning on staying the same?

Heck, I don't use the same lip balm every day. Change is a *good* thing.

Marriage is an opportunity to reinvent who you are, not because you don't like who you are, but because you want to become an even more glorious version of yourself.

We all have things we'd like to change about ourselves, so why not use this new life as a way to start things on the right foot?

I tell brides (and grooms) that this is a great time to commit to growing and improving themselves. Not only are they changing for themselves, but they're also becoming a better partner in the process.

Yes, you're both going to change, but if you've committed to changing for the better, everyone wins.

Especially you.

Ten simple ideas... to Reinvent yourself

- ◆ Make a list of goals for this year, next year, and the year after.

- ◆ Create couple goals. You can both achieve them in different ways or with the support of the other.

- ◆ Take a class. Go back to school.

- ◆ Try a new sport.

- ◆ Volunteer at a local charity organization.

- ◆ Run a race. Or walk.

- ◆ Learn a new language.

- ◆ Go to a new place without reading up on it in a travel guide.

- ◆ Dye your hair. (Or something that radically changes your appearance. Just for fun.)

- ◆ Get rid of old clothes, old books, old ideas, and old patterns.

38. You get what you give

"For it is in giving that we receive."

- FRANCIS OF ASSISI

Your marriage isn't about getting everything you want, but about getting everything that you need.

ally

I am a romantic. Let's get that out there. And you probably are, too. The second you are in a marriage, you believe that everyone will just know what to say, what to do, and everything will be magical bliss.

Cue the contented sigh.

But we're human. We have needs when we're in a relationship, some that we share and some that we don't.

And, even though we don't want to admit it, relationships are often a tug-of-war because one person thinks they should get *all* of the attention.

But ... so does the other person.

Or, one person gives and gives and gives of themselves, with the expectation that they will get something in return. And that can backfire.

My advice is that you should go into a marriage without wanting or expecting anything.

When you don't want, you aren't stuck in the cycle of *me*. Plus, when you add in the attitude of wanting to give, you are creating a positive and healthy relationship.

And marriage.

Think about one of your best friends. Chances are good that you don't expect her (or him) to be anything else but themselves. And because you love them, you are willing to help them and to give your best to them.

This extends to your marriage, too.

When you give love, you will get love.

This happens in the reverse, too. If you give bitchiness, you get bitchiness. And yes, we all have those days. No one is asking (or telling) you to be perfect.

What you want to do is to become more conscious of how you act in your relationship.

If you want more, give more. If you want change, you need to change.

If you want love, you need to give love.

Your marriage becomes the result of what you put into it. For better or for worse.

Ten simple ideas... to Give to your marriage

- Put yourself in your partner's shoes.

- Don't take everything personally. Sometimes, a bad day for your partner isn't about you.

- Think about how you can make your love smile.

- Hide notes in your partner's wallet, purse, computer or office.

- Surprise your partner with dinner or flowers or something they'd actually enjoy.

- Take your partner away for a day or a weekend. Tell no one.

- Listen to your partner when they need to be heard.

- Always support your partner's right to make their own decisions, even if you don't agree.

- Make time for your partner and they will make time for you.

- Don't keep score in your marriage.

39. Joy is easier to wrap

> "There are those who give with joy,
> and that joy is their reward."
>
> - KHALIL GIBRAN

Memories don't fade, unless we allow them to.
We can hold onto our memories tightly
by documenting what we have
experienced during our lives.

Ally

Gray hair, wrinkles, sagging parts no one wants to think about. (And don't head to the mirror right now.)

Your memory is going to fail you at some point, and you may not even realize it. (Funny how that works, isn't it?)

Beyond the clichés of throwing your keys in the freezer and forgetting where you parked at the mall, it's not just the everyday things that will escape us at some point.

It's the big things, too.

But you can capture your memories and trap them in places where you can visit them again and again.

It's not just the photos you take (and have taken), but you can also find other ways to save this day in your mind.

One of my favorite things was a bride who saved all of the ribbons from the wedding and hung them in her home during the holidays.

The ribbons that were on the centerpieces were turned into trimmings for the tree, ribbons for the wreaths, and special touches for the bride and groom's home.

Or the bride who burned a music playlist that she played again and again on her wedding anniversary.

You're not going to remember everything, but you can save reminders and those reminders will bring you back to the day whenever you want to remember it.

Yes, lovely, you're going to grow old and your brain is going to grow old. Thankfully, you're growing old with someone special.

I'm not trying to make you feel bad, and I'm not telling you that you should be worried about being old, because there are many beautiful ways to make your wedding stay vivid in your mind.

Your memories stay when you want them to stay, when you make sure they're a part of your life forever.

All it takes is a little creativity and documentation. Not the boring kind, I assure you.

♦ Take photos, before, during, and after the wedding.

♦ Use a voice recorder to capture your thoughts during the big day.

♦ Keep the music playlist from your wedding and replay it.

♦ Take videos of your wedding ceremony and the reception (maybe even the risqué parts!).

♦ Save pieces of your décor and put them around your home.

♦ Distribute items from your wedding for others to enjoy in their homes (i.e., give decorations to others to hang on their holiday trees.)

♦ Scrapbook your wedding, using programs, invitations, and so on.

♦ Make up a wedding box with your favorite bits from your wedding.

♦ Have a book for your guests to fill out at your wedding, including advice for married life.

♦ Take pictures of your families, friends, and loved ones. Hang the photos in your home.

40. What's your story, Morning Glory?

> "There is no greater agony than
> bearing an untold story inside you."
>
> - MAYA ANGELOU

*Your wedding is more than just a big party.
It can become a story of love that you tell
your loved ones. And yourself.*

Ally

I love a good love story, don't you? No matter how many times I tell my own love story, I still get a little misty-eyed.

What's your story?

The day of your wedding can also be a story, a story that is told and retold for years to come – and not just by you. The way you express your love, your relationship, and your interests during a wedding tell you a story.

Think about it this way:

1. **The first meeting** – This starts to happen when your guests arrive at your wedding. They're slightly nervous and they're excited about what's to come.

2. **The first kiss** – I'd call this the culmination of the wedding vows and a kiss between the two getting married.

3. **Falling in love** – The reception can be a celebration of the interaction between the bride and the groom and the people in their lives.

4. **The relationship** – At the end of the night, when things are wrapping up and goodbyes are said, this is the commitment to love from this day forward.

Throughout this process, you're telling a story for the guests, and it might just be a story of what's happening in the moment, or it could be a story of your love.

But each moment of your day can contribute to this story.

Think about this – a good storyteller keeps you engaged and eager to learn more. During your wedding planning, think about how the guests will feel with each new event and moment.

Are they still interested in turning the page to find out more?

By expressing your story in a positive way, in an uplifting way, you create a story that guests then become a part of.

You create a story in which your guests can experience joy and happiness with you.

You might feel comfortable telling the actual story of how you met and fell in love. Or you might want to create a story for the night that encapsulates your love – for example, a fairy tale wedding might begin with the couple arriving in a carriage, then going to the wedding, then being at the reception, and then driving away.

Now, storytelling doesn't have to be elaborate (or expensive).

All you need to do is to think about how you can have your wedding create a story for the guests to follow.

Create a page-turner.

I know you will.

Ten simple ideas... to tell your Story well

- ◆ Write out your love story.

- ◆ Talk to your love about how they see the story of the wedding day.

- ◆ Create a schedule for the day to see if there are any "missing pages."

- ◆ Walk yourself through the wedding through the eyes of a guest.

- ◆ Use exciting moments to start new chapters of the wedding day.

- ◆ Share the day's story with guests before, during, or after the wedding, so they can remember it.

- ◆ Think of a story to act out as a part of the wedding.

- ◆ Post photos of your relationship's love story.

- ◆ Tell the story of how you met to your guests.

- ◆ Continue telling the story of your wedding – i.e., in the thank-you notes, in a marriage update on a wedding website, and so on.

Acknowledgments

A little thank you ...

I am a "save the best for last" kind of girl. Here is my best thank you to ...

Alec and Jillian, for being my inspiration and making all things meaningful. Thank you for being my endless source of joy and for being patient with me. Mama is still learning.

Carol, my God-given best friend, thank you for relentlessly speaking into me and changing my life. (Trust me. Totally hot.)

Jennifer, my partner in crime, the "girly girl" in my life, thank you for being right by my side.

Ed and Rachel, for believing and seeing the real "Ally."

Jinger, Katrina, Jon, Dave, Mike, Lynda and Kent, my "A" Team. Thank you for bringing "underwear" to life.

Courtney, Brittney, Cali, Bailey and Sarah – in your absence, I would be a "fashion don't." Thank you for showing up and hanging out on this wild adventure.

To Mom and Dad, and to our entire family – thank you for loving me and showing me that crazy is beautiful.

And lastly …

Dedication

to my Love, Aqua Man

Without you I would be huddled in a horrible fluorescent-light office with pasty-white walls, tortured by my never-ending list of things I *think* I need to do. Thank you for giving me the courage to get my hands dirty, jump out of perfectly good airplanes, learn how to water-ski and still love me even when I want to "induce labor."

Thank you for being perfect "breeding stock" for beautiful smart babies. Thank you for showing them how a man loves a mermaid.

Thank you for being a father to many and having the heart of a superhero. Thank you for listening to all of my scary thoughts and endless conversation about what I think matters.

Last, but not least, thank you for being willing to let me change my mind, my outfits, and our bedroom paint every couple of years, and saving me from wearing really bad "granny" underwear.

I love you ... and your fast boats.

Ally

About Ally

In 1990 Alexis Asbe founded one of northern California's leading wedding and special event companies, and has worked on more than 3000 events. Her work has been featured on Extreme Make-Over Home Edition and in Modern Bride magazine.

With more than 20 years in the design and art business, Alexis has worked with celebrities, royalty and everyone in between. She is devoted to health, love, and family, and she is hopelessly addicted to the stuff that really matters ... which drives her husband *crazy*.

Find out more at *www.allyasbe.com*

Love Notes

Love Notes

Love Notes

Love Notes

Love Notes

COMING SOON

Cooking in your UNDERWEAR

What ~~he~~ *we* really want~~s~~